BALING OUT

BALING OUT

AMAZING DRAMAS OF MILITARY FLYING

Robert Jackson

First published in Great Britain in 2006 by
PEN & SWORD MILITARY
an imprint of
Pen & Sword Books Limited
47 Church Street
Barnsley
South Yorkshire
S70 2AS

ISBN: 1 84415 347 9
ISBN: 978 1 84415 347 3

A CIP catalogue record for this book
is available from the British Library

Typeset in Sabon by Pen & Sword Books Limited

Printed and bound in England by
CPI UK

Pen & Sword Books incorporates the imprints of
Pen & Sword Aviation, Pen & Sword Naval, Pen & Sword Military,
Pen & Sword Select, Pen & Sword Military Classics,
Leo Cooper and Wharncliffe Books

For a complete list of Pen & Sword titles please contact:
PEN & SWORD BOOKS LIMITED
47 Church Street, Barnsley, South Yorkshire, S70 2AS, England
email: enquiries@pen-and-sword.co.uk
website: www.pen-and-sword.co.uk

Contents

BIBLIOGRAPHY

Air Ministry, *Airborne Forces*, Air Historical Branch, 1951

Carter, Nick, *Meteor Eject*, Woodfield Publishing, 2001

Bowman, Gerald, *Jump for it! Stories of the Caterpillar Club*, Evans Brothers, 1955

Dorr, Robert F. and Bishop, Chris, *Vietnam Air War Debrief*, Aerospace Publishing, 1996

LeBow, Eileen F., *A Grandstand Seat: the American Balloon Service in World War I*, Greenwood, 1998

Hay, 'Doddy', *Man in the Hot Seat*, Collins, 1969

Jackson, Robert, *Arnhem: the Battle Remembered*, Airlife, 1994

Jackson, Robert, *Spitfire: the Combat History*, Airlife, 1995

Jackson, Robert, *Hawker Hunter*, Ian Allan, 1982

Jackson, Robert, *Sea Harrier and AV-8B*, Blandford, 1989

Jackson, Robert, *Air War Flanders, 1918*, Airlife, 1998

Jackson, Robert, *Canberra – the Operational Record*, Airlife, 1988

Jackson, Robert, *The High Cold War*, PSL, 1998

Jackson, Robert, *Air War over Korea*, Ian Allan, 1973

Jackson, Robert, *The Jet Age*, St Martin's Press, Inc, 1980

Lucas, John, *The Big Umbrella*, Elm Tree Books, 1973

Mackersey, Ian, *Into the Silk: True Stories of the Caterpillar Club*, Robert Hale, 1956

Philpott, Bryan, *Eject, Eject*, Ian Allan, 1989

Sharman, Sarah, *Sir James Martin: the Authorised Biography*, PSL, 1996

Smith, J.R. and Kay, A.L., *German Aircraft of the Second World War*, Putnam, 1972

CHAPTER ONE

EARLY PARACHUTE DEVELOPMENT

The world's first documented parachute was actually intended to be a flying machine. In 852, a Moor named Armen Firman jumped from a tower in Cordoba, Spain, using a loose cloak stiffened with wooden struts in an attempt to perform a gliding flight. The apparatus only succeeded in arresting his fall, making it a kind of parachute, and Firman walked away with only minor injuries. In 1178, another Muslim attempted a similar feat in Constantinople, but he broke several bones and later died of his injuries.

The Chinese, too, experimented with parachute-like devices. The first recorded successful quasi-parachute jumps were made in China in 1306, as part of the celebrations during the coronation of the Emperor Fo-Kin. Leonardo da Vinci sketched a parachute while he was living in Milan around 1485. However, the idea of the parachute may not have originated with him: the historian Lynn White discovered an anonymous Italian manuscript from about 1470 that depicts two designs for a parachute, one of which is very similar to da Vinci's. The first known test of such a parachute was made in 1617 in Venice by the Croatian inventor Faust Vrancic (also known as Fausto Veranzio), who constructed a device based on Da Vinci's drawing and jumped from a Venice tower in 1617. Vrancic published a work entitled *Machinae Novae*, in which he described in text and pictures fifty-six advanced technical constructions, including his parachute, which he called the *Homo Volans* (Flying Man). The device consisted of a square cloth attached to a frame, the corners of which were tied to a body harness.

Other accounts of quasi-parachute descents include one by a Monsieur de la Loubères, who, during a visit to Siam (Thailand) in 1687, gave a detailed description of an athlete who entertained the King of Siam and his courtiers by jumping from a height under two umbrellas, the handles of which were attached to his belt.

In 1783, a Frenchman, Sebastien Le Normand, jumped from an observation tower at Montpellier under a braced conical canopy 2 feet 6 inches in diameter. The vertical distance covered was probably 30 feet. A more positive step in the history of parachuting was made a few years later by another Frenchman, Jean Pierre Blanchard.

Jean Pierre François Blanchard was born on 4 July 1753 in Petit Andelys, France. He began inventing a variety of interesting devices as a young boy, including a rat trap with a pistol, a velocipede, and later a hydraulic pump system that raised water 400 feet from the River Seine to the Château

Gaillard. He also attempted to develop a manually powered aircraft and helicopter but was unsuccessful. During the 1770s Blanchard worked on designing heavier-than-air flying machines, including one based on a theory of rowing in the air currents with oars and a tiller.

However, Blanchard was best known for his many pioneering balloon flights. He took up ballooning following the Montgolfier brothers' 1783 demonstrations of hot-air-balloon flying in Annonay, and made his first successful ascent in a balloon he built himself on 2 March 1784. On 7 January 1785, Blanchard and Dr. John Jeffries, an American physician, made the first flight over the English Channel, travelling from Dover to Calais. In the same year, Blanchard gave the first successful demonstration of the use of a parachute when a basket containing a small animal was dropped from a balloon and parachuted to earth. In 1793 he claimed to have made a parachute descent at Basle, Switzerland, after the hot-air balloon in which he was travelling exploded, but he landed heavily and broke a leg. The claim was never corroborated, and it is more likely that he came down in the balloon's gondola, with the deflating balloon itself acting as a kind of parachute. In February 1808, Blanchard suffered a heart attack on a flight over The Hague in the Netherlands and fell more than 50 feet. He never recovered from the fall and died on 7 March 1809. By an ironic twist of fate, Blanchard's widow was also killed in a balloon accident; on 7 July 1819, she met her death when her hydrogen balloon ignited and exploded during a firework display at the Tivoli Gardens, Paris.

Blanchard, it should be noted, developed the first foldable parachute made from silk. Before that, all parachutes were made from rigid frames. It was left to another Frenchman, though, to demonstrate the first use of a parachute without a rigid frame. He was André Jacques Garnerin, who was born in Paris on 31 January, 1769. He studied physics before joining the French Army and over the next few years became interested in hot-air balloons and their potential use for military purposes. Garnerin began experimenting with parachutes while he was a prisoner of war in Hungary, the idea being that he might use such a device to escape from the ramparts of the prison fortress where he was being held, but he never got the opportunity to put his theory into practice. It was not until 1797 that he completed his first parachute: consisting of a white canvas canopy 23 feet in diameter, it had 36 ribs and lines and was semi-rigid, resembling a very large umbrella.

Garnerin made his first successful parachute jump over Paris on 22 October, 1797. After ascending to an altitude of 2230 feet over the parc Monceau in a hydrogen balloon he jumped from the basket. As the inventor had failed to include an air vent at the top of his parachute, he oscillated wildly in his descent, but despite this design flaw he landed unhurt half a mile from the balloon's take-off site. Garnerin therefore became the first man to design a parachute that was capable of slowing a man's fall from a high altitude.

In 1799, Garnerin's wife, Jeanne-Genevieve Garnerin, became the first woman to make a parachute jump. Garnerin made exhibition jumps all over Europe including one of 8000 feet in England on 21 September 1802. He was injured during the descent when a strap supporting the basket snapped. André Jacques Garnerin died in Paris on 18 August 1823 when a wooden beam fell on his head as he was preparing equipment prior to a balloon launch.

The demonstrations made by Garnerin convinced other aeronauts that the carriage of parachutes might be a good idea. It certainly proved to be a good thing for Polish balloonist Jordarki Kuparanto, who, on 24 July 1808, baled out of a Montgolfier-type balloon that had caught fire over Warsaw.

It was another decade before the parachute was first demonstrated in America. The man involved was Charles Guille, who on 2 August 1819 jumped from a hydrogen balloon at a height of about 8000 feet and landed safely at New Brunswick, Long Island, New York.

The problem of oscillation during a descent greatly exercised the minds of parachute designers, and it would be many years before it was realised that the matter could be resolved by the addition of a simple vent at the top of the canopy. One inventor who thought he had the answer was Robert Cocking, a professional watercolourist and amateur scientist, who spent many years developing an improved design for a parachute after witnessing Garnerin's parachute descent in 1802. On 24 July 1837, Cocking arranged a trial of his invention from the Vauxhall Gardens in London. The parachute, which took the form of an inverted cone connected by three hoops, was attached to Charles Green's 'Royal Vauxhall' hydrogen balloon, piloted

Robert Cocking, who lost his life in 1837 when his conical parachute folded up. Often described as a young man, Cocking was in fact 61 years old. (Science Museum)

by Green and Edward Spencer. When the balloon reached 5000 feet, Cocking gave the order to Charles Green, who released his parachute. The canopy was covered with linen and used stiffeners made of thin metal tubes to retain its shape,but it was heavy, weighing 223 pounds. It worked quite well at first, but then the stiffening tubes started to give way and a hole developed in the canopy, which collapsed. Cocking, suspended in a basket underneath, plunged to earth and died soon after hitting the ground, becoming the world's first parachute fatality. Despite Cocking's tragic failure, a German named Lorenz Hengler is said to have made several trouble-free jumps with a conical parachute from heights of between ninety and 350 feet.

The man who might justifiably be described as the father of the modern parachute was an American, Captain Thomas Scott Baldwin, who was credited with inventing the first parachute harness. Born in Missouri in 1854, and orphaned at an early age, he became an acrobat at fourteen with a travelling circus and then began to set his sights on aviation. He made his first balloon ascent in 1875 and for the next ten years made thousands more at country fairs and exhibitions all over the United States. Searching for something more daring, he re-invented the rigid parachute, redesigned it and made it flexible so it could be packed. Then he offered to jump from a balloon, the going rate being a dollar for every foot of his descent. On 30 January, 1885, Baldwin ascended to a height of 1000 feet over San Francisco's Golden Gate Park, perched on a small seat under the balloon with his legs dangling in space. Then, before an enthralled and horrified audience, he ripped open the balloon and started his earthward plunge, opening his parachute after a few seconds of free fall.

In 1900, Baldwin set out to improve his act and began investigating dirigible balloons. Using a motorcycle engine built by Glenn Hammond Curtiss and an elongated balloon, Baldwin designed and built the dirigible California Arrow, which flew the first circuitous flight in America on 3 August 1904. The Army Signal Corps became interested in the airship idea and offered to pay him $10,000 for a practical means of dirigible aerial navigation. Baldwin built a dirigible that was 95 feet long and powered by a newly-designed Curtiss engine. The Army purchased it and designated it SC-1 (Signal Corps Dirigible Number 1).

In 1910 Baldwin built his own aircraft, the first to feature an all-steel framework rather than wood, and called it the Red Devil. It was powered by a 60 horsepower Hall-Scott engine. He formed a troupe of aerial performers and toured several countries in the Far East, making the first aircraft flights in many of them. In 1914 he returned temporarily to dirigible design and development, creating the US Navy's first successful dirigible, the DN-1. He then began training heavier-than-air pilots and managed the Curtiss School at Newport News, Virginia. One of his students was the young Billy Mitchell, later to become a great advocate and champion of American military air power.

Captain Thomas Scott Baldwin at the controls of his aircraft, the Red Devil. (via John Scott)

When the United States entered the First World War, Baldwin volunteered his services to the Army, even though he was 62 years old. He was commissioned a captain in the Aviation Section of the Signal Corps and appointed Chief of Army Balloon Inspection and Production. Consequently, he personally inspected every lighter-than-air craft built for, and used by, the Army during the war. He was promoted to the rank of major during the war. After the war he joined the Goodyear Tire and Rubber Company in Akron, Ohio, as a designer and manufacturer of airships. He died in 1923 at the age of 68, having made an enormous contribution to aviation.

In 1890, Paul Letteman and Käthe Paulus, two German exhibition jumpers, developed the concept of folding the parachute into a knapsack-like container, reducing its bulk. Paulus also demonstrated the 'breakaway' technique, in which a parachute was inflated and, on being released, pulled open a second.

The first recognised parachute jump from an aircraft occurred on 1 March 1912, when Captain Albert Berry jumped from a Benoist aircraft flown by Anthony Jannus at 1500 feet over Jefferson Barracks, St Louis, Missouri. Berry had a 36-foot parachute packed into a metal case beneath the fuselage; it was fitted with a trapeze bar for him to sit on as he descended, clinging to the suspension lines. Some sources, however, give the credit for the first aircraft jump to an exhibition jumper called Grant Morton. Late in 1911, Morton is reported to have jumped from a Wright Model B aircraft flying over Venice Beach, California. Morton carried his folded parachute in his arms; as he jumped he threw his canopy into the air. The parachute opened, and Morton landed safely.

These parachutes and all others used before them were of the automatic type, meaning that they were either inflated prior to the jump or were pulled into the airstream from a container fastened to the aerial platform. This type of parachute, however, soon proved to be inadequate for safe escape from moving aerial platforms. In 1908, Leo Stevens devised the first parachute which could be opened by the jumper with a ripcord, although the 'free' type parachute was not utilised substantially until 1920.

A patent granted early in 1911 to an Italian inventor named Pino for a flexible parachute, including a pilot chute, must be considered as one of the major milestones in parachute history. A jumper using this new device could wear his parachute in a pack like a knapsack. On his head would be a hat-like device fashioned into a leather cap, which would blossom out into a smaller open parachute. During the jump, the small pilot chute would pull off the hat and deploy the larger parachute from the knapsack.

The first freefall jump was made by a remarkable woman called Georgia 'Tiny' Broadwick in 1914. She was called 'Tiny' because she weighed only 85 pounds and was a mere 4 feet tall. Georgia became the first woman to jump from an aircraft on 21 June 1913, when Glenn L. Martin dropped her from 2000 feet above Griffith Park in Los Angeles, California. Broadwick was also the first woman to make an over-water jump from an aircraft, and was also the first woman to jump from a seaplane. In 1941 Georgia gave the first demonstration of a parachute jump to the U.S. government and subsequently made several more, the first four being static line jumps. She nearly came to grief on the fourth jump, when the static line became entangled with the aircraft, so on later jumps she made the line much shorter, making it just long enough for her to clear the aircraft before pulling the parachute open. Georgia Broadwick died in 1979.

Although parachutes were successfully demonstrated many times in the early years of the twentieth century, their use was slow to be appreciated in military circles. Even the outbreak of the First World War, with its widespread use of aircraft and airships, did little to awaken interest. It was the deployment of the observation balloon by both sides that finally brought about a change of attitude.

The diminutive Georgia 'Tiny' Broadwick about to make a parachute jump in 1914. (via John Scott)

CHAPTER TWO

THE 1914-18 WAR

In the early months of the war, the fluid nature of the fighting had precluded the use of observation balloons on a large scale, although the Germans used them to good effect on the Ypres front in October 1914, as is recorded in *A Popular History of the Great War.*

> *Saturday, October 30, broke over the Ypres front in mist. A low ground fog had prevailed throughout most of the previous ten days' fighting, but the mist on this day was lighter. Indeed, by 10 a.m. it had quite dispersed and for the first time the Germans were able to use their captive observation balloons to direct their artillery. This increased visibility gave the superior German guns a further advantage, and its effect was to be felt throughout the day.*

The French and Belgians also used balloons for artillery observation during these early months. The RFC, having laid emphasis on more modern technology such as wireless telegraphy for artillery co-operation, had no balloons to deploy, and in May 1915 the French obligingly loaned one to the British I Corps to assist in artillery spotting during the second Battle of Ypres. A sausage-shaped kite balloon, with stabilising fins that enabled it to operate even in adverse wind conditions and a basket suspended underneath to accommodate one or more observers, it generated enough interest at HQ BEF for a request for help to be sent to the Admiralty, the Royal Navy Air Service (RNAS) having assumed responsibility for all lighter-than-air craft in 1913. The RNAS deployed a number of kite balloons to the front and these were operated under Royal Flying Corps (RFC) control in 1915, but the RNAS continued to provide support and equipment until July 1916, when the War Office decided that it was time the RFC had its own balloons, and placed contracts accordingly.

The first Kite Balloon Section to be made available by the Admiralty was assigned to V Corps, and was first in action over Poperinghe on 25 May, 1915. Another balloon section reached France on 26 June and was deployed in the same sector as its predecessor on 1 July. Back in England, the Polo grounds at Roehampton were requisitioned to provide facilities for a Balloon Training Centre.

By the end of June 1916 a long line of kite balloons was in position on both sides of the lines, their observers constantly reporting enemy dispositions and movements in preparation for the great battle that was about to develop on the Somme. Some observers on the front of the British Fourth Army had a bad time when their balloons were struck by lightning in a fierce thunderstorm that raged on Friday, 23 June. One balloon tore loose, carrying its occupants to a height of 13,000 feet (3965m) over the German lines before it drifted back again and descended to earth. Both men escaped with their lives, although one

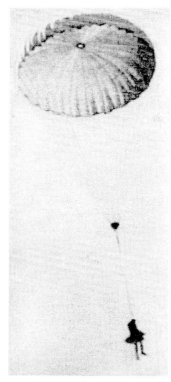

A balloon observer, coat billowing, makes his escape by parachute after his kite balloon came under attack. (National Archives)

was badly frost-bitten. During this period, observation balloons were the object of frequent attacks, as the official history records:

Two balloons were destroyed by No 60 Squadron, but in this the hopes of the RFC exceeded its achievement. The German balloons were not only very heavily defended, they were also hauled down as soon as the attacking aircraft were sighted. Two pilots of No 60 Squadron, Ball [Captain Albert Ball, later to be awarded the VC – author] and Lieutenant A.M. Walters, were among those sent to destroy balloons with Le Prieur rockets, mounted on the outside struts and fired electrically. Finding that their quarries had gone to ground they joined in an air battle and sought to use their rockets against a Roland and an LVG. Ball missed, but got his man with Lewis gun fire, while Walters had the satisfaction of hitting the LVG with one of his rockets and sending it to the earth in flames.

Our own balloons were very active; one of them of No 3 Section was moved in the afternoon to the outskirts of Montauban, where it was soon found that the cable attaching it to earth was in the direct line of fire of one of our heavy batteries. Nevertheless, the observer preferred to accept the risk and continued his observations, until what was feared happened. A shell cut the cable, the balloon soared away and, having ripped it, the observer regained contact with the ground by parachute.

Although of poor quality, this photograph of a BE.2c clearly shows the rails for the Le Prieur rockets which were used to attack enemy balloons. (Author's collection)

German balloon observers were equipped with a parachute designed by the noted female parachutist Käthe Paulus and worn as a pack on the observer's back. British and French observers had parachutes packed in conical containers attached to the balloon's basket and linked to the occupants by static lines. Parachutes were relatively primitive with a failure rate of approximately one in a hundred. The parachute harness itself was not government issue, and would be made up locally for each individual observer. One observer, Captain Machin, better known as the cartoonist Mac, recalled that 'Our self-made harness of Willesden canvas, strongly stitched by a corporal fitter, was a waist belt and cross-shoulder pieces attached by trouser buttons'. Attached to this was a rope which trailed over the side to the parachute suspended in the balloon rigging. An additional hazard to survival was the observers' dress: they generally wore heavy chromed leather coats and thigh length sheepskin lined 'fug' boots to combat the cold. The harness arrangement was cumbersome, and the shoulder straps had a tendency to slip off if the wearer bent forward.

One Royal Flying Corps observer who was killed through parachute or harness failure was the music hall star Basil Hallam Radford, better known by his stage name of Basil Hallam, a man who was famous in his day. Prevented from joining the infantry at the outbreak of war because of a steel plate in his leg, the result of an old injury, he joined the Royal Flying Corps in the summer of 1915 and, after completing his training at Roehampton, he was appointed as a balloon officer on 20 September. After further training he was posted to France and joined No 3 Army Kite Balloon Section on 9 June 1916. Six days later he was appointed Flight Commander to No 1 Army Kite Balloon Section. Only two months later, he was dead.

In his obituary *The Times* stated that,

> *The balloon in which he was observing broke away, and, having thrown all the papers overboard, he tried to descend by parachute. It failed to open, and he received fatal injuries.*

The full circumstances of his death, however, appear to be a little more complicated than this simple story suggests. On 20 August 1916, with Second Lieutenant P.B. Moxon, Captain Radford ascended in a Caquot kite balloon behind Beaumont Hamel, a location from which they could observe over the mills and railway stations of the Avere Valley through to Thiepval. Late in the afternoon, while registering artillery for V Corps, the cable broke, either because it suffered overstrain after being wound too tightly, or because it was severed by a shell, and released from its moorings the Caquot drifted off. After some delay Lieutenant Moxon was seen to jump to safety, but Captain Radford fell minus his parachute, landing on the Aucheux road.

A good account of the perils of balloon observing, and its attendant parachute escape, was given by an unnamed officer in the American publication *Illustrated War News* of January 1918.

> *Brown and I had been warned overnight that it was our turn for 'sausage observation' and with the accuracy of a mental alarm-clock, my*

brain woke me exactly at daybreak. With a shiver and a half-formed hope that it would be misty – in which case I could sneak another hour between the blankets – I poked my head out of the door and scanned the weather sign some four miles away. Long experience has taught us that the four skeleton walls of the ruined farm-house on the sky-line are as good visibility indicators as can possibly be obtained therefore we call them our weather sign.

But this morning they stand out clear and sharp against the grey sky, not a trace of mist anywhere near them, and, with a groan, I withdraw my head, shake Brown into some sort of consciousness, and perform a hasty toilet. Then, with cigarette well alight, go out to seek the flight-sergeant, who, smart and dapper and jaunty, has already dressed and waits my orders. The sturdy fellows draw the sausage-shaped gasbag from its shed, and walk it down to the ascension ground, carting the winch after it, and generally preparing it for the day's work. Meanwhile, in a corner of a smoky mess-room, Brown and I are stowing away vast quantities of porridge and bacon. We smoke a last cigarette as we stroll to the ascension ground, where the Intelligence officer awaits us with the chart. This scrutinised, and the work to be done explained thoroughly, we don the attachments for the parachutes, strapping them on firmly, for upon their security may depend our lives.

The balloon is toggled on to the rope of the winch, and, stepping inside, we examine basket, valve and ripping-cords, and ballast and then make fast our parachutes – practically getting into our lifeboats before our ship is properly launched.

'Right – ease out!' cries Brown, he being the senior officer. The sergeant blows his whistle once, cries 'Let up hand over hand !' and as the air-mechanics gradually ease out on the half-dozen ninety-foot ropes the 'sausage' begins gradually to ascend. When we reach the end of these ropes the winch commences slowly to revolve, and its giant cable holds us in reluctant leash as we gradually rise heavenwards.

Five hundred feet, and the first stop. The balloon is bucketing about like a kite in a gale in the twelve-mile-an-hour wind we stop to measure. We halt and gauge the wind velocity at every 500 feet until we reach the 3000 mark, at which altitude our work is done. Sometimes we find that a heavy ground mist obscures the earth and spoils our visibility and with many curses, we descend once more, having been to quite a lot of trouble for nothing. But if we can get a good view of the ground all around our batteries, and of the trenches of the opposing side we commence operations forthwith.

The enemy's shells are a source of interest to us. We are called upon to report the distance they are falling beyond or short of their targets, which are usually our own heavy-gun emplacements; and, in addition, we must give the nature of the shell – whether it is the soft, fleecy-clouded shrapnel or the yellowy-brown amatol, the black cloud of *lyddite or the deadly grey-green of the gas-shell. And though we are perched so high above the world, well behind even our own lines and safe from the too-pressing attentions of 'Archies', life isn't exactly one sweet song for us, nor yet a dull existence. In fact, we get far too many thrills.*

There was the occasion when a Boche aeroplane came our way one day and tried to set us alight with machine-gun fire. We had nothing but our automatic pistols for defence, but we used these to good effect, and had the pleasure of seeing the Hun crash to the ground – it was afterwards ascertained that a pistol bullet had passed through his heart and killed him as he sat at the controls.

Then another day, we had front seats at as pretty an air-fight as one could wish to see. Again it was a Boche who had penetrated our lines, and his antagonist was a young aviator only three days out from the base school. Round and round us they flew, both eager for the combat, and their machine-gun bullets hummed and shrilled round our ears like so many bees. They weren't close enough to us for our pistols to carry, or we might have taken a hand. But in the end, the youngster scored his first aerial victory and the marauding Boche met with a sudden and incandescent death.

On a third occasion we were attacked by an enemy airman, and this time he not only set the balloon afire, but severed the winch-cable with his machine-gun bullets, so that the 'sausage' was drifting away on the high wind a mass of flame.

We had to jump quick that time, I can assure you, and as I fell, my parachute refused to open. In an instant of time all the horrors of crashing to the ground to be broken to pulp flitted through my mind; all the stories of defective parachutes and aerial accidents with their gruesome details affrighted my very soul and I said my prayers with the swiftness of a machine-gun. Then I felt a jerk that almost broke my back and with exasperating slowness, the umbrella of the parachute opened and checked my downward rush.

I was little more than a ghost when I at length reached earth in perfect safety, and though my nerves were all in rags, I was compelled to lie down on the ground and roll with laughter at the sight of my confrère. His parachute had acted from the first, and now he was hanging head downwards on the branch of an adjacent tree, apostrophising with vivid profanity all the Boches that fly, and all the air mechanics in our own service; the first because through one he had got into his present predicament, the second because they didn't help him down fast enough for his liking.

There was the time when a sudden gust of wind tore the cable out of its hold, and sent us careering at over 8000 feet for the north. We could see, in the rifts of the clouds, the earth speeding past at express rate, but soon the darkness hid that and we knew what it felt like to be in a raiding

Zeppelin when it had broken down. We expected every minute that the aerial defences of England would open fire upon us, for we knew the course upon which we were drifting, but though searchlights were out at various towns none picked us up – the clouds screened us too effectually. All that night we drifted and just before dawn felt a terrific bump that stopped the balloon. Trying for soundings, we found ourselves well aground and managed to climb down out of the basket after ripping the envelope. And, when dawn came, we found we had grounded on one of the mountains of the Pennine chain – had drifted from somewhere in France to a quiet little village in Derbyshire.

Flight Sergeant W.S. Lewis, who served with the RFC and Royal Air Force from 1915 as a balloon observer, had an even more hair-raising parachute experience. He told his story in *Everyman at War* (Ed C.B. Purdom, 1930).

In the early part of May 1916, before the big Vimy Ridge battle, in the morning soon after sunrise the balloon ascended with Lieutenant H. and myself to about 5000 feet. Everything was at peace except an anti-aircraft gun showing evident anger at an annoying mosquito that was buzzing over enemy country. That bark was the only sound that made one realise that a tragic war was on. For people with jaded nerves who are perplexed with the ceaseless hurry, bustle, and noise of modern life, I recommend a few hours up aloft in a kite balloon as a tonic and respite from its cares and worries. There is a charming and attractive calm and quietness about the experience that is recuperative and restful...

Our object on this morning was to locate a very annoying gun that kept everybody in our sector of the front on tenterhooks by its back-area firing – a nasty irritating business.

We nicknamed the gun 'Ginger', and its explosive crumps gave everyone the jumps. A hollow bang would faintly be heard in the distance, and, before you could count two, with a terrific whoop and crump, a high explosive shell would burst near.

We were out to locate this gun, but for a long time Lieutenant H. and I did not trouble much about guns. We were too enraptured with the glorious sunrise. It was wonderful, marvellous – words fail me to express what I felt. I felt very near to what some people call the infinite, whatever they may mean, or, as some may say, near to God, but whatever it was I was thinking and feeling, I began to realise in some dim way that to be absorbed in a vision of unutterable beauty is a fine experience. I was thinking that it was good to have been born, just to experience that one thing. I thought of many other things in a rambling sort of way...

Bang! Like a big drum being struck. Swish-rip – a sighing whistle, a noise, or rather a shriek like the tearing of some gigantic piece of canvas. Christ! What's happened? Gee! The balloon has burst. It had collapsed about us, and we were coming down. I desperately struggled to push away the fabric of the balloon from the basket, and suddenly from underneath the mountain of fabric, I glimpsed the white face of Lieutenant H.

'We must jump,' he said. I agreed with him, and immediately dived over head first, and nearly dived through my harness. It had no shoulder straps, only a waistband and loops for one's legs. Never shall I forget that sickening horrible sensation when, in my first rush through the air, I felt my leg loops at the knees, and my waistband round my buttocks. I managed, however, to grab hold of the thick rope which is toggled on from the waistband to the parachute. Meanwhile, everything else seemed to go wrong; the cords of the parachute somehow in the struggle got entangled round my neck, so that as the parachute began to open with a deadly pull on my body, I was literally being strangled in mid-air.

The sensation was horrible and unforgettable; my face seemed to swell to twice its size, and my eyeballs to become too big for their sockets. Then I was suddenly freed, and could breathe again, but my neck was badly lacerated and raw. My bad luck was not over, however, because I was suddenly pulled up with a sharp jerk that jarred every bone in my body.

I had fouled the cable which held the balloon to the winch, and my parachute had, in striking it, coiled itself round about three or four times. Suspended in mid-air! I remained in that helpless position for what seemed like hours, and I looked down, and saw Lieutenant H., his parachute getting smaller and smaller. Then I slowly began to unwind – round and round I went like a cork, and broke away with a rush, the silk of my parachute being torn almost across, and I began hurtling down at a great speed, with my damaged and useless parachute flap, flap, flapping above me.

I thought it was all up with me. I had seen a couple of parachute accidents, and I knew what to expect. I could do nothing but curse at the damned bad luck I was having. I have read that face after face of one's friends and scenes of one's past haunt one when in danger. It is perfectly true, because I actually experienced it.

Crash! I had shut my eyes, I thought I had struck the ground. No; in a slanting, rushing dive, I had struck poor old H.'s parachute, and the force of my fall had caused his parachute to collapse.

'Sorry,' I shouted. One had to shout I remember, for the wind seemed to be blowing a gale, although actually it was a calm, sunny day. 'Sorry, but I couldn't help it.'

'It's all right, old man,' he shouted, 'but couldn't you find some other bloody patch to fall on? Millions of bloody acres about you, yet you must pick me to fall on.' 'It looks like finish,' he continued. It did.

Suddenly his parachute began to bellow out with a flapping roar, tumbling me off like a feather, but I was too inextricably bound up with his cords to shoot away altogether; incidentally, I was hanging like grim death to something or other. What it was I don't know, but I imagine it was about half a dozen of his parachute cords. And so we landed, two on one parachute. At least, I landed first, because I seemed to slip down just before we landed, and he landed full weight on top of me.

I know nothing of what happened immediately after, but I heard *subsequently that we had landed almost on the support trenches, and scores of Canadians had rushed out and gathered round us, and that the enemy thought it was a fine opportunity to drop a few shells around.*

Captain Eddie Rickenbacker, who became the leading US air ace of the First World War with twenty-six victories, witnessed balloon observers parachuting to safety:

A sudden flare of flames struck my sight off to the right. Running around the trees I caught a view of one of our balloons between me and Thiaucourt completely immersed in flames! Half-way down was a graceful little parachute, beneath which swung the observer as he settled slowly to Mother Earth!

And as I gazed I saw a second balloon two or three miles further east towards Pont-A-Mousson perform the same manoeuvre. Another of our observers was making the same perilous jump! A sly Heinie had slipped across our lines and had made a successful attack upon the two balloons and had made a clean getaway. I saw him climbing up away from the furious gale of anti-aircraft fire which our gunners were speeding after him. I am afraid my sympathies were almost entirely with the airman as I watched the murderous bursting of Archy all around his machine. At any rate I realised exactly how he was feeling, with his mixture of satisfaction over the success of his undertaking and of panic over the deadly mess of shrapnel about him.

In half an hour I arrived at the balloon site and found them already preparing to go aloft with a second balloon. And at my first question they smiled and told me they had seen my Fokker of this morning's combat crash in flames. They readily signed the necessary papers to this effect, thus constituting the required confirmation for my last victory. But for the victory of yesterday that I claimed they told me none of the officers were present who had been there on duty at that time. I must go to the 3rd Balloon Company just north of Pont-a-Mousson and there I would find the men I wanted to see.

After watching the new balloon get safely launched with a fresh observer in the basket, a process which consumed some ten or fifteen minutes, I retraced my steps and made my way back to my motor. The observer whom I had seen descending under his parachute had in the meantime made his return to his company headquarters. He was unhurt and quite enthusiastic over the splendid landing he had made in the trees. Incidentally, I learned that but two or three such forced descents by parachute from a flaming balloon are permitted to any one observer. These jumps are not always so simple, and frequently, very serious if not fatal injuries are received in the parachute jump. Seldom does one officer care to risk himself in a balloon basket after his third jump. And this fear for his own safety limits very naturally his service and bravery in that trying business. The American record in this perilous profession is held, I believe, by Lieutenant Phelps of New York, who made five successive jumps from a flaming balloon.

The winches to which observation balloons were attached were initially steam operated and mounted on horse-drawn trucks, but by 1918 they were mostly petrol-driven. The early winches were capable of hauling a balloon down at 200 feet per minute, but later winches achieved six times this rate of descent. A great many observers were forced to part company with their balloons when menaced by air attack; the 2nd Balloon Wing RFC alone made 106 emergency parachute descents in one year of operations at the front, two officers, Captain T.G.G. Bolitho and Second Lieutenant H. Cresswell, each making four descents. Mostly the parachutes worked, but sometimes they did not, as Lieutenant Smith of No 29 Balloon Section found to his cost on 19 June 1918. With Flight Sergeant Shepherd – who was seriously wounded in the back during the attack – he took to his parachute after their balloon was set on fire by an enemy aircraft. Shepherd's parachute opened but Smith's did not. He fell for several hundred feet, crashed through the branches of a tree and fell into a bog, from which he emerged with no more than a severe shaking.

Neither was a fully deployed parachute a guarantee of survival, as fighter pilots were not above taking pot-shots at enemy balloon observers. The official RAF communiqué for 4 September 1918 records that:

> *Captain T.F. Hazell, 24 Sqn, brought down two hostile balloons in flames, one of which fell on the winch which burned for 20 minutes and Lt E.P. Crossen attacked the observer whose parachute collapsed.*

In the summer of 1918 a certain disaffection began to spread among the RAF's aircrews because of the unnecessary suffering and loss of life caused by the failure

Doomed to die. This photograph, although heavily retouched, is nevertheless genuine and shows what appears to be a French Spad fighter falling in flames. The pilot's only alternative to a painful end was to jump clear. (Author's collection)

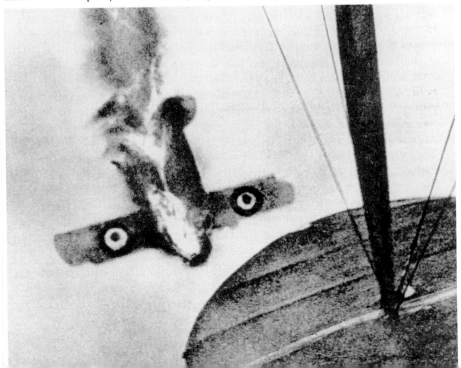

of the authorities to issue parachutes to flying personnel. In the early days, primitive parachutes were bulky and heavy, and to wear them would have imposed an unacceptable weight penalty, as well as restricting the pilot's movements. But by 1918, more powerful aero-engines and improved parachute design had done away with such objections, and the RAF's doctrine that the wearing of parachutes would be detrimental to the aggressive spirit of its pilots was frankly nonsensical; exactly the opposite would have been true. One of the RAF's leading air fighters, Lieutenant (later Wing Commander) Ira Jones, writing of an air battle that took place on 1 June 1918, summed up the general feeling:

> For ten minutes the ten S.E.s engaged the seven Pfalz; and when the battle ended one enemy had gone down in flames, one had crashed, and one had gone down out of control... while we had lost our flight commander (Captain W.J. Cairns). A determined Pfalz got to within 25 yards of him and gave him the gun. His right wing was suddenly seen to break up, the nose of his S.E. dipped viciously, then downwards he spun at a terrific rate. I watched him for a short while, sickness overcoming me. It is a terrible thing to see a pal going to his death... I cannot imagine why we have no parachutes.

The RFC had, in fact, been experimenting with parachutes designed for use by aircraft crews for nearly two years. On 13 January 1917, after twenty drops with dummies had proved the system, Captain C.F. Collett had made the first live jump from a British aircraft, making his exit from a BE.2c at 600 feet and landing safely. Even before the war, a parachute for aircrew had been developed by a retired engineer, R.E. Calthrop, who called it the 'Guardian Angel'. He informed the Royal Flying Corps of his invention and successful tests were carried out by Mervyn O'Gorman, Superintendent of the Royal Aircraft Factory at Farnborough.

Despite encouraging test results, Sir David Henderson, Commander of the RFC, was unwilling to give permission for them to be issued to his pilots. Pressure was also applied on Calthrop not to publicise his invention. With growing numbers of pilots losing their lives as a result of their inability to parachute from a crippled aircraft, Calthorp rebelled and in 1917 advertised his Guardian Angel parachute in several aeronautical journals. He revealed details of the tests that had been carried out by the Royal Flying Corps and pointed out that British pilots were willing to buy their own parachutes but were being denied the right to use them.

The Air Board responded to Calthrop's adverts by setting up a committee to look into the possibility of allowing RFC pilots to use parachutes. Although some members of the committee favoured their use, the Air Board decided against the measure. Officially the reason given was that the Guardian Angel was not 100% safe, it was too bulky to be stored by the pilot and its weight would affect the performance of the aeroplane. Unofficially the reason was given in a report that was not published at the time:

> It is the opinion of the board that the presence of such an apparatus might impair the fighting spirit of pilots and cause them to abandon

machines which might otherwise be capable of returning to base for repair.

This opinion prevailed almost until the end of the war, when the Air Ministry relented and ordered 500 Guardian Angels, together with 500 parachutes of other types. By then it was too late for a great many pilots and observers.

The fact that enemy pilots were often seen to jump from doomed aircraft and parachute to safety in the closing months of the war did nothing to help the morale of Allied pilots, either, as these extracts from the official communiqué show.

August 11th. Lt C.V. Gardner, 19 Sqn, attacked one of four Pfalz scouts, which fell in flames. The pilot of this machine was seen to jump out and go down in a parachute.

August 12th. In the evening, Capt C.H.R. Lagesse, leading a patrol of 29 Sqn, saw four Fokker biplanes above him, and after outclimbing, attacked the leader... and shot him down. Lt C.J. Venter attacked another of the EA (enemy aircraft), which burst into flames. The pilot of this machine stalled and jumped out, and was seen to go down and land in a parachute.

But the parachutes did not always work, or suffered some mishap:

September 7th. Captain M.E. Ashton and Lt T.D. Fitzsimon, 12 Squadron, attacked an LVG which, after 50 rounds had been fired by the observer, fell out of control and crashed. The observer of the hostile machine was seen to jump out about 100 feet from the ground, but his parachute did not open.

September 8th. Captain G.B. Gates, 202 Squadron, engaged an Albatros two-seater which turned over on its back and caught fire. The observer jumped out in a parachute which, however, also caught fire.

November 4th. A formation of 211 Squadron, while on photographic reconnaissance, was attacked by a formation of EA, whose leader was fired on by the pilots and observers of two machines... this EA went on fire and broke up, the pilot leaving the machine in a parachute which did not open.

One pilot whose parachute did work was the legendary Ernst Udet, Germany's second-ranking air ace with sixty-two victories. On the morning of 29 June 1918 Udet took off in his Fokker D.VII to intercept a French Breguet two-seater, which was directing artillery fire over the lines. Approaching the Breguet with great skill and precision, he fired at the observer, who sank into his cockpit. Now Udet casually swung around for a side shot at the helpless Breguet, targeting the engine and pilot. Suddenly the observer sprang up and manned his machine gun, sending a long burst of bullets into Udet's Fokker, wrecking his machine gun and controls so that the aircraft would only fly in circles. He made a vain effort to bring it under control, but it fell away in a spin from which he could not recover.

Udet stood up in the cockpit to bale out. However, the slipstream blew him over the side, but instead of tumbling clear of the aircraft he was brought up

Ernst Udet pictured in his later years. He committed suicide in 1941. (National Archives)

sharply by a sudden jolt and realised to his horror that his harness was caught on the rudder. Frantically, he struggled to free himself as the earth spun closer.

Suddenly the Fokker nosed down into a spin from which Udet could not pull out. He was wearing one of the new Heinecke parachutes that German pilots were just being equipped with, and frantically, he struggled with the harness and managed to free himself at a height of a few hundred feet, landing safely in no-man's land. He quickly scrambled back to the German lines and, taking his harrowing experience in his stride, was flying again that same afternoon. The next day he shot down a Spad fighter for his 36th victory.

An excellent account of what it was like to bale out of a doomed aircraft in the First World War was provided by Lieutenant Frigyes Hefty of the Austro-Hungarian Air Corps. On the morning of 22 August, 1918, 24-year-old Hefty, a pilot with the 42nd Fighter Squadron, took off from Pianzano, on the Piave river, in his Albatros D.III. He was strapped into a Heinecke parachute, the first time he had worn one.

Over the Piave at 14,000 feet, Hefty became involved in a dogfight with some Italian Hanriot HD-1 fighters. His Albatros was hit and set on fire.

Fire was always the biggest dread of the combat pilot of the First World War, and as flames licked up through the floorboards, I found myself in a dizzy whirlpool of mixed feelings – fear, desperation, impotence and the will to survive. I subconsciously fired my twin Spandaus and pulled up the nose of my Albatros in an attempt to break through the circle of Hanriots, but my aircraft suddenly fell away out of control. The controls did not respond to my frenzied movements. The cables had either been damaged by machine gun fire or burned through, and the Albatros lurched drunkenly, flames now licking up towards my face.

I tried to hoist myself out of the cockpit – anything was better than this scorching inferno. I was stuck! Desperately I tore at the safety belt. I could not see it for the all-enveloping flames. The flames were already penetrating my leather face mask and I could smell my moustache singeing. I thought I was burning to death.

I screamed in terror as, with a final effort, I tore the buckle of the safety belt open and thrust my head above the flames. I stood up, grasped the upper wing, kicked the stick over and, as the crippled Albatros rolled over on its back, I was vaulted into the void. I tumbled over and over, and had a momentary glimpse of my faithful old Albatros diving steeply, trailing a banner of red flames and black smoke.

I jerked the release of the contraption that had made my flight so uncomfortable. Suddenly my headlong fall was checked as, with a crack, the chute blossomed open. There was a terrible pressure on my chest and I gasped for air. The world seemed to have gone mad, a vast grey mass whirling round and round. What was wrong? Had the heat damaged my sight? Then I realised that my charred goggles were obscuring my vision. The cold, rarified air cleared my head a little, and I became aware that my waist-belt had slipped up around my chest when the chute opened. I manoeuvred my legs until I could get my left foot through a loosely hanging leg strap. I forced myself into an upright position and, with my remaining strength, lifted myself up so that the belt was once again around my waist, thrusting my left arm through the belt so that it would not slip again. I was still gyrating madly and, looking up, I saw the reason to be the faulty packing of the chute. One of the shroud lines ran across the canopy, dividing it into two.

I tried to check my position, and it looked as though I was drifting towards the Italian lines. I began to suffer a feeling of acute melancholy coupled with one of complete detachment, probably brought on by the strange silence. Now the chute began to sway, and the Piave seemed to be coming nearer. Could it be the wind? The shroud lines began to hum like a harp, and the Alps were now towering above me. I began to realise how rapidly I was descending. Then I heard the staccato rattle of machine guns and, almost simultaneously, the roar of a rotary engine. I turned my head, and my feeling of detachment left me. One of the Italian Hanriots had returned and its pilot was now firing at my parachute.

I hung limply, hoping he would believe me to be already dead, and then everything turned grey as I dropped into a layer of cloud. At times the chute swung madly, and I felt a series of updraughts followed by hard, downward jolts. Now I seemed to be falling even faster, and as I fell free of the cloud, the ground seemed to rush towards me. I swung dizzily from side to side, trying desperately to focus my eyes on the ground below. I saw a broad highway lined with trees, vineyards and stone walls – typical Italian scenery. Soldiers were running in the general direction of what seemed likely to be my point of impact. Then a tall maple barred my descent. I struggled to work my left arm free of the waist-belt, but it was numbed, and, with a splintering and cracking, I was falling through the tree's branches. I felt a stabbing pain in my ankle, and then merciful oblivion... I opened my eyes and found myself lying under the huge maple. The smiling faces of Hungarian infantrymen peered down at me. So that new-fangled parachute really did work!

In 1918, No 3 Squadron RAF pioneered a technique which was to prove of enormous value in future operations: the dropping by parachute of small arms ammunition to Allied troops in newly-captured positions, saving the infantry a lot of effort and risk. Using information gleaned from a captured enemy document, the bomb racks of the R.E.8s were fitted with clips to hold two boxes each containing 2000 rounds of .303 ammunition, above which were metal canisters for the packed parachutes. The latter were made of aeroplane fabric, with a fourteen-foot diameter and a one-foot hole at the top. The observer released the boxes by means of a Bowden cable and their weight pulled the parachutes from the canisters. Trial drops were made in June by No 3 Squadron's Captain L.J. Wackett, and were so successful that the technique was quickly adopted by the RAF's army co-operation squadrons. On 4 July, No 9 Squadron RAF, operating from Flesselles, was detailed to drop ammunition to forward troops of the 4th Australian Division east of Nieppe. As the advance developed the troops marked the main dropping points with a white 'N', while individual machine gun posts requiring ammunition displayed the letter 'V'. The operation was carried out in close co-operation with No 3 Squadron. Just before dawn on the 4th, the whole squadron flew low over Hamel, dropping bombs and generally making as much noise as possible to cover the sounds of the advancing Australian Corps. The attack was over in a short time, with remarkably light casualties, and in mid-morning No 9 Squadron began its supply-dropping activities, Major J.R. Rodwell's twelve R.E.8s averaging four thirty-minute sorties to drop ninety-three boxes totalling 111,600 rounds on six aiming points. Refuelling and reloading – the latter carried out by a specially-trained team of sixteen men – had averaged twenty minutes. Eight of the R.E.s had supplied the main positions, while the other four had assisted the machine gunners. The average dropping height was 200 feet. Inevitably, there had been a cost. Two of the low-flying R.E.s, braving intense enemy machine gun fire to deliver their loads, were shot down and their crews killed. They had begun a tradition which was to reach its highest and most tragic hour of gallantry over a quarter of a century later, at Arnhem.

Apart from saving balloon observers and aircrew fortunate enough to have them, and for dropping supplies, parachutes were used for one other purpose. Towards the end of the war, many secret agents were dropped by parachute rather than landed. In the summer of 1918, the Canadian pilot Major W.G. Barker, who was later to win the Victoria Cross for a gallant single-handed dogfight against fifty enemy aircraft over Flanders, set out from an Italian airfield in an Airco DH.4 to drop an Italian agent named Tandura behind the Austrian lines. The plan was to land the man in some remote area from which he could make his way to Vittorio, collecting as much military information as possible en route and transmitting it by carrier pigeon to the Italian forces.

Barker and Tandura were accompanied by a Captain Wedgwood Benn (later to become 1st Viscount Stansgate and father of the Rt Hon Antony Wedgwood Benn, MP) who was to act as navigator and despatcher. Three

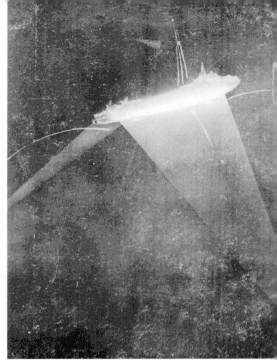

No second chance. The Germans issued parachutes to their airship crews in the latter months of the war, but it was too late for many who met a fiery end in earlier attacks on the British Isles. These two impressions show Zeppelin L.34 coned by searchlights and under attack by 2nd Lt Pyott of No 36 Squadron over Hartlepool Bay in November 1916. (Author's collection)

Actual photograph of the end of Kapitänleutnant Max Dietrich's L.34. As the blazing tangle of wreckage fell from the sky, some of the crew jumped clear rather than be burned alive. (Author's collection)

Another photograph of a Zeppelin's demise – this time the L.31, shot down at Potter's Bar, Essex, by 2nd Lt W.J. Tempest of No 39 Squadron in October 1916. (Author's collection)

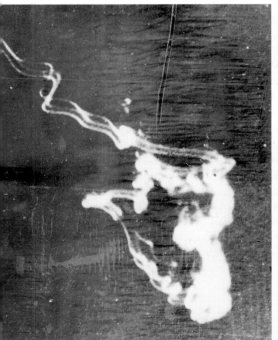

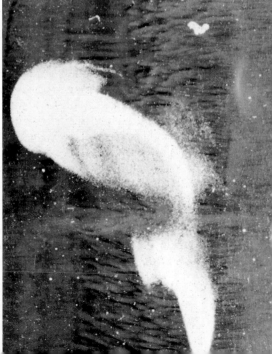

bombs were also carried, two of them to be dropped after the agent had been released and the third to be retained in the machine as proof that Barker and Benn had been engaged on what Benn later decribed as 'a legitimate act of war' should they be forced down in enemy territory.

Tandura, a tough little mountaineer, wore Italian Army uniform but carried peasant's clothing in a knapsack. Following a safe landing, he operated behind the enemy lines from August to October 1918, gathering information of such value that the Italians regarded him as one of the principal architects of their success in the Battle of Vittorio and awarded him the Gold Medal for Valour, the Italian Army's highest decoration for gallantry.

Since parachuting was a new science in the First World War, some agents were understandably afraid to launch themselves into space and place their trust in a thin silken canopy. The pilots of No 60 Squadron RAF, who – despite being fighter pilots in a unit equipped with SE.5s – were sometimes called upon to drop agents from elderly BE and FE aircraft in 1918 and they overcame this problem by making the agent sit on a trapdoor in the fuselage floor. When the pilot pulled a toggle, the trapdoor opened and the agent fell through. There was one story of a terrified agent, clinging to the sides of the cockpit for dear life, being beaten over the fingers with the butt of the pilot's pistol until he eventually let go.

CHAPTER THREE

THE INTER-WAR YEARS

I t was General William 'Billy' Mitchell, Commander of the US Air Service in France, who was primarily instrumental in getting an organised parachute test and development programme started in the United States. As a result of his pleas for more and better parachutes for his pilots, a parachute facility was established at McCook Field, Dayton, Ohio, and began functioning in the summer of 1918. In December 1918, Major E.L. Hoffman was put in charge of the project, which had now assumed considerable importance.

Initially, experiments at McCook Field were conducted on automatic parachutes of two general types. In the first, the parachute and its container were attached to the aircraft, and the parachute was connected by a line to a harness worn by the jumper; in the other, the parachute was packed in a bag, worn by the jumper, and the line connected the parachute directly to the aircraft. In both cases, the pilot or jumper had only to jump, and when he reached the end of the rope, the parachute was automatically pulled out of its container and into the airstream. Great difficulties were experienced during attempts to perfect this type of parachute deployment, and although hundreds of tests were conducted with these models, none met the rigorous requirements which had been established.

Thoughts turned once more to a 'free' parachute to be released from the pack by the operator after he jumped. The first model, known as Model-A,

A trainee parachutist jumps from the wing of a Martin MB.2 bomber over McCook Field, Ohio. (US Army)

was 28 feet in diameter, and comprised a flat circular parachute canopy made of straight-cut silk. It was composed of 40 gores with 40 braided suspension lines and had a vent 40 inches in diameter controlled by thick rubber bands. It was packed in a back-type pack. This model was later altered to a 24-foot diameter canopy in a seat-type pack. Considerable effort was expended on the development of the free parachute; on 28 April 1919, after a number of successful dummy tests, it was tested in a live jump from an altitude of 1500 feet.

The parachute used in this test was developed by Leslie Irvin and Floyd Smith, and it was Irvin who made the test jump. He pulled the ripcord as soon as he cleared the aircraft, an Airco DH.4, and the canopy became fully deployed at 1000 feet.

More than 1,500 successful experimental parachute jumps were made from aircraft before the seat pack type parachute was issued as regular equipment to the U.S. Army Air Service in 1919. In 1922, use of the parachute became mandatory by order of the Adjutant General. On 20 October 1922, Lieutenant Harold Harris, Chief of the Flight Test Section of the Engineering Division of the U.S. Army Air Service, took off in a Loening PW-2A monoplane from McCook Field to test the experimental balanced ailerons that had been fitted the previous day. While engaged in a manoeuvrability test against a Thomas Morse MB-3, piloted by Lt Muir Fairchild, Lt Harris suddenly experienced a terrible vibration in the aircraft's controls. Unable to regain control of the stick, he opted to jump out and use his parachute. After erroneously pulling on the leg strap fitting three times, he found the correct handle and pulled it at 500 feet off the ground, landing in the back garden of 337 Troy Street, in Dayton, Ohio. His was the first life ever saved in an emergency jump from a disabled aircraft with a manually operated parachute. Harris later became a general, and unsurprisingly retained an active interest in flight safety to the end of his career.

Lt Harold Harris, who became the first man ever to save his life with a manually-operated parachute in October 1922. (US Army)

When he retired in June 1966, he was Chairman of the Flight Safety Foundation Board.

Harris's experience led to the foundation of the 'Caterpillar Club', an exclusive organisation whose members, all of whom had saved their lives by Irvin parachute, were entitled to wear a little gold (later gilt) caterpillar pin, the Caterpillar being symbolic of the silk worm, which lets itself descend gently to earth from a height by spinning a silk thread upon which it hangs.

By 1939, membership of the Caterpillar Club stood at about 4000; six years later, at the end of the Second World War, it had risen to 34,000, and the estimated figure in 2005 was over 100,000.

The architect of Harris's survival, Leslie Leroy Irvin, was born in Los Angeles, California on 10 September, 1895. Irvin's interest in aviation began while he was working as a stuntman for the film industry in California, where he had to perform acrobatics and descents from hot air balloons. In 1914 he was eventually hired to jump from 1000 feet into the sea from an aircraft using a standard balloon parachute. Early in 1918 Irvin identified the need for a reliable parachute for aviators and began to put his own ideas on life-saving parachutes into practice. The exact specifications of the first parachute that Leslie made are not recorded. What is known is that it was a static-line operated back-pack; that it incorporated a harness of original but somewhat uncomfortable design; that the canopy was made from cotton; and that it worked. We know that it worked because Irvin himself jumped with it several times during the spring and summer of 1918.

On 18 June, 1919, a Certificate of Incorporation was issued and the Irving Air Chute Company was born. A clerical error resulted in the addition of the 'g' to Irvin and this was left in place until 1970, when the company was unified under the title Irvin Industries Incorporated.

Other air forces across the world were now keenly interested in the parachute, not least the Royal Air Force, whose leadership had at last woken up to the fact that its pilots' lives were valuable. The RAF squadron principally involved in parachute trials was No 12, which had formed part of the Army of Occupation in the Rhineland after the Armistice. It was the last operational squadron in Germany, disbanding on 22 July 1922. In 1923, the Royal Air Force began a limited expansion programme and 12 Squadron was reformed at Northolt on 1 April that year. The Squadron was equipped with DH 9As, and during the year expanded to full 3-flight strength. In March 1924, 12 Squadron moved to Andover and co-located with No 13 (Army Co-operation) Squadron. It was at this time that the Squadron re-equipped with the Fairey Fawn, a two-seat day bomber fitted with the Napier Lion engine.

Over the next few years, the Squadron settled down to a peacetime routine, which consisted of the annual training programme, along with several trials and displays. The annual training programme, in principle, began with individual training in the autumn and worked round to Squadron training in the summer consisting of bombing, formation flying, navigation exercises and gunnery. The trials carried out included some limited night flying and the introduction into service and testing of parachutes for aircrew. This involved a number of practice jumps being performed by observers, who would climb out of the aircraft onto a small ladder and await a signal from the pilot as the aircraft flew over the airfield at 2000 feet. The observers carried no reserve parachutes, and the silk material from which the parachutes were constructed had a tendency to build up a static charge whilst in storage, so that when the ripcord was pulled, the silk stuck together. Sometimes, the result was that the

Much experimental parachute work in Britain was carried out with the Airco (de Havilland) DH.9A, which was the workhorse of the RAF in the 1920s. (Author's collection)

canopy 'roman candled' and failed to deploy, with disastrous consequences for the jumper.

The first parachute to be standardised by the U.S. Army Air Corps, after considerable development effort and experimental testing, was of the seat type, for use by both pilots and other crew members. It consisted of a pack containing a flat circular solid-cloth canopy, 24 feet in diameter, incorporating a three-point harness release. It was given the designation S-1, and became standard in 1926. One year later, a second seat-type parachute was standardised under the designation S-2. It retained all the features of the S-1 parachute, except that it used a flat circular solid-cloth canopy 28 feet in diameter, to ensure the safe descent of somewhat heavier crew members. By this time, several other applications for the parachute, apart from insuring the safe escape of crew members, became apparent, and there was now a requirement to develop parachutes for such specific applications as airborne forces and supply dropping.

In 1929 Major Hoffman, who was in charge of the parachute unit at

Wilbur Wright Field, Dayton, Ohio, started the development of a radically new triangular type of parachute canopy. In 1932, the triangular canopy was standardised and adapted into a seat-type parachute, the S-3. It was also developed into the first training parachute, the C-1, which was a combination of seat and back type, and into the first attachable chest parachute, the A-1, which could be quickly clipped on to its harness by crew members. Also in 1929, the quick-release mechanism was patented in Great Britain and subsequently manufactured in the United States by the Irving Air Chute Company. Prior to the introduction of the quick-release device, jumpers risked serious injury by being dragged along the ground after landing, or drowning in the event of a water landing as they struggled to free themselves.

There were many notable parachute escapes during the inter-war years. One of the luckiest involved Ernst Udet, whose parachute had saved his life in 1918. Nearly two decades later, he was test-flying the Heinkel He 118 prototype dive-bomber, which was in competition with the Junkers Ju 87 for a lucrative government contract. On 27 July, 1936, Udet took off in the Heinkel He 118 V-1, which bore the civil registration D-UKYM, to carry out some high-speed dives over Lake Müritz. As Udet was on the point of pulling out, the propeller inadvertently feathered itself, the fast reduction of the rpm sheared the toothed wheels in the reduction gear, the engine tore away from its mountings and the aircraft literally broke up around him. His seat belt broke and he struggled clear of the wreckage, opening his parachute a couple of thousand feet above the ground. He received slight injuries on landing.

Surrounded as they were by struts and bracing wires, pilots of the inter-war biplanes often had difficulty in escaping from the cockpit of a crippled aircraft. It happened to Pilot Officer Robert Stanford Tuck early in 1938. Tuck was the pilot of one of three Gloster Gladiator biplane fighters of No 65 Squadron RAF Hornchurch, practising tight formation flying at 3000 feet. The aircraft were in line astern formation, each aircraft a little above and a shade to the right of the one in front. Tuck, a newly commissioned pilot officer, was flying number three at the end of the line.

Suddenly the three biplanes hit a patch of severe turbulence which caused the middle aircraft, flown by Flight Sergeant Geoffrey Gaskell, to buck wildly. The pilot over-corrected and his aeroplane slewed to the left and then dropped into the slipstream of the leading Gladiator. Tuck, flying behind, was poised, ready to yank the stick over and get out of the way if the number two aircraft failed to get back into position very quickly. But the pilot, who could have broken to the left into empty sky, unaccountably hauled his aircraft up and broke to the right.

Tuck saw him rear up, directly ahead. There was no time for avoiding action. The two machines were, for an instant, poised at right-angles to one another and Tuck found himself looking down into the other pilot's cockpit. Then, with a noise like that of a splintering tree, came the collision. Tuck's propeller sheared through the fuselage of the other aircraft and his windscreen was instantly covered with writhing sheets of fabric and buckling airframe. The wings of his aircraft folded up and wrapped themselves about the fuselage, covering Tuck's cockpit like a shroud. The wreckage, with Tuck trapped inside, began plummeting towards the earth.

Bob Tuck now began a desperate struggle to get out of his plunging aircraft. He tried to slide back his cockpit canopy, but the folded wings held it fast and it refused to budge. He smashed at the canopy with his fists, tearing at it with his fingers until the nails were ripped off and his hands sticky with blood, but the canopy remained unyielding. Then came the terror. A blood-red veil clouded Tuck's brain and he found himself yelling and cursing in a strange, inhuman voice.

Bob Stanford Tuck pictured in the cockpit of his Hawker Hurricane fighter in 1940, with 23 'kills' stencilled under the cockpit. His score rose to 29 before he was shot down and taken prisoner. (IWM)

Suddenly, the brilliant glare of daylight flooded the cockpit once again and startled the young pilot from his momentary panic. The wreckage which had held him prisoner was wrenched from the canopy by the slipstream, and as it went it took the canopy with it. Tuck seized his chance. A brief, violent struggle against the centrifugal forces and he was plucked from the cockpit like a cork from a bottle. His parachute opened with just 300 feet to spare. After he landed, Tuck found that his right cheek had been slashed by a bracing wire, leaving him with a long scar which he would carry for the rest of his life. Tuck eventually became a wing commander and one of the RAF's leading fighter aces, gaining 29 victories before his Spitfire was shot down over France in January 1942. This time he crash-landed, and spent the rest of the war in various prison camps. He died in May 1987, aged 70.

The inter-war years witnessed a very important development in the story of the parachute: the formation of airborne forces. The first true paratroop drop

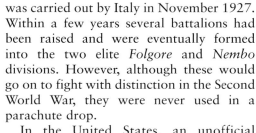

was carried out by Italy in November 1927. Within a few years several battalions had been raised and were eventually formed into the two elite *Folgore* and *Nembo* divisions. However, although these would go on to fight with distinction in the Second World War, they were never used in a parachute drop.

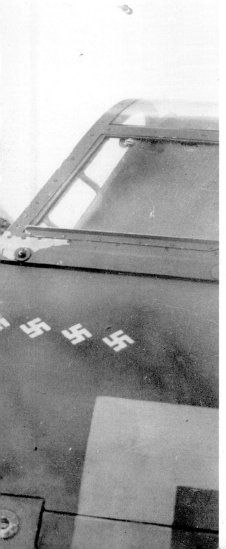

In the United States, an unofficial paratroop training programme was launched at the instigation of General Billy Mitchell as far back as the autumn of 1928, when six armed parachutists jumped from a Martin bomber over Kelly Field, Texas. This demonstration, however, was regarded as nothing more than a stunt, and although limited experimentation continued, it was not until the spring of 1940 that the United States established an official paratroop training programme at Fort Benning, Georgia. The first troop-type parachute (T-1) consisted of two ripcord-opened packs, attached permanently to a single harness with two sets of risers; a back pack containing a 28 feet flat circular solid-cloth canopy; and a chest pack containing a 22 feet flat, circular canopy. During subsequent modifications, harness webbing of a lighter weight was substituted (T-3), and initiation of deployment was changed

Soviet paratroops jumping from a Tupolev TB-3 bomber/transport. Experiments were also carried out in which paratroops jumped without parachutes into snowdrifts from a TB-3 flying slowly at low altitude. Casualties were sustained not through impact injuries, but suffocation. (IWM)

The Junkers Ju 52/3m, seen here in civilian markings, remained the mainstay of Germany's airborne forces throughout the 1939-45 war. (Lufthansa)

from ripcord actuation to static-line actuation (T-4).

It was the Soviet Union that led the way in the development of an operational airborne force. In 1930, a parachute detachment of one officer and eight men was dropped during manoeuvres to surprise, attack and capture an 'enemy' headquarters, and on 18 August, 1933, in a demonstration near Moscow forty-six paratroops jumped from Tupolev TB-3 aircraft, a small 1.7-ton T-27 armoured car also being dropped under a large parachute from a cradle under the fuselage of one of the aircraft. On 1 March 1935, two infantry battalions totalling 700 men were dropped at Kiev, and three gliders each carrying eighteen passengers landed after being triple-towed for 1170 miles. All the glider pilots, and the pilots of the towing aircraft, were women. This was followed, during manoeuvres held in Byelorussia in 1936, by a mass drop of 1200 paratroops at Minsk with full equipment, while transport aircraft landed a further 2500 men. The manoeuvres were witnessed by a British Military Mission led by General (later Field Marshal Lord) Wavell. In their report the Mission remarked that although this demonstration was a most spectacular performance, the use of parachutes was of doubtful tactical value. Nevertheless, in 1937, the Committee of Imperial Defence took note of the possibility of airborne raids being made on this country in time of war, but thought that the danger of such raids on any considerable scale was, at that time, negligible.

There were those in Nazi Germany who held a very different view, and who by 1937 were well on the way to organising a viable combat force of paratroops. Already, in 1933, Hermann Göring had formed a small paratroop unit from men of a police unit known as *Landespolizeigruppe* Berlin, which was to be used as a special force to combat communist activities within German cities. On 1st April 1935, this unit was renamed Regiment General Göring.

Early in 1936 a trials team of about fifteen officers and sixty to eighty other ranks under the command of a Major Immanns was formed at Stendal to review the feasibility of paratroop operations and to assess what form of exercises and practice jumps were to be employed. On 11 May 1936, Major Bruno Oswald Bräuer made the first parachute jump from a wing of a Klemm KL25 sporting aircraft and became the first German *Fallschirmjäger* to be given a *Fallschirmschützenschein* (parachuting licence).

The target for each parachute unit was to carry out five day-jumps and one at night using the RZ1 parachute. The aircraft would be the Junkers Ju 52 and jump height would be about 400 feet. On 4 October 1936, the first public demonstration of a military parachute jump in Germany took place at Bückeberg, south of Hameln, when thirty-six *Fallschirmjäger* under the command of *Oberleutnant* Kroh, jumped from three Ju 52 transport aircraft.

By the spring of 1937 it had definitely been decided to use an automatic parachute (in other words, one attached to an aircraft by a static line), and a system of training was developed. A parachute training school was formed at

Stendal in February 1937 under the command of *Generalmajor* Gerhard Bassenge, a *Luftwaffe* officer and First World War fighter ace with seven victories. Bassenge's proposals for the future use of parachute troops were as follows:

a. A parachute battalion was to be trained as a special demolition unit and used against objectives such as railways, bridges, power lines, high tension lines and so on. The logic behind this proposal was that objectives of this nature could normally only be destroyed by using strong bomber forces, whereas by dropping demolition troops, usually under cover of darkness, the destruction could be carried out with greater economy.

b. A parachute battalion of the Army was to be formed, consisting of a Headquarters, a Signals Platoon, three Rifle Companies and one Heavy Company; then two parachute battalions were to be created with the object of forming a Parachute Infantry Regiment and finally a Parachute Infantry Division. These forces were to be used in conjunction with Army operations and were to form part of the Army, which would control their training, equipment and organisation.

c. A Transport Group was to be formed, comprising three squadrons, each of thirty-six aircraft, and it was proposed that this group remained exclusively at the disposal of the army parachute units for peacetime training. In the event of mobilisation, it was to be reinforced with transport aircraft and brought up to the strength of a transport air division.

Probably because of rivalry between the *Luftwaffe* and the Army, Bassenge received no decision on his proposal. Nevertheless, the Parachute School at Stendal was confirmed in its status and received authority to train both *Luftwaffe* and Army personnel; it was also permitted to create an experimental department and to issue orders to industry on behalf of the *Wehrmacht*.

Airborne forces took part in German Army manoeuvres in the autumn of 1937, a parachute demolition force of fourteen squads being dropped in night operations against railway lines and communications in West Prussia and Pomerania. The paratroops carried out their tasks successfully and were unobserved by the 'enemy'. Also in 1937, a DFS 230 assault glider was demonstrated before a gathering of senior German officers, the glider, piloted by Hanna Reitsch, casting off from a Ju 52/3m at about 3000 feet and landing virtually at the feet of the assembled officers. Within seconds, eight fully armed soldiers had disembarked and taken up combat positions. During the autumn of 1938 a small glider assault command was formed under *Leutnant* Weiss, and it was found that the use of glider-borne troops had many advantage over those dropped by parachute. Their approach was silent, they were not dispersed and they did not have to spend precious time extricating themselves from parachutes.

By the summer of 1938 the Parachute School at Stendal had expanded to a strength of twelve companies, with about 180 parachute instructors. Courses normally lasted for two months and the school's peacetime capacity was over 4000 a year. The eventual wartime capacity was over twice this number.

On 29 May 1938, a conference with Hitler took place in Berlin in which the military situations and intentions were discussed in view of forthcoming operations in the Sudetenland, and *Generalmajor* Bassenge was ordered to equip, organise and train an airborne force to be employed against Czechoslovakia in the autumn. At this time both the *Luftwaffe* and the Army had their own individual parachute forces, and Bassenge was ordered to train both to the highest standard. Air transport units were also to be reinforced, equipped and trained. Tactical command of the airborne force was assigned to *Generalmajor* Kurt Student, and it was given the title of 7 *Fliegerdivision*, with a strength of some 9000 men supported by eight transport groups with 250 Junkers 52s and a small glider echelon with twelve DFS 230s. Although it was not required in the annexation of the Sudetenland, one battalion took part in a demonstration drop into a field in the occupied zone. Hermann Göring witnessed this drop and was so impressed that he told Student of his intention to form an Airborne Corps. The promise was never fulfilled.

The next task allotted to 7 *Fliegerdivision* was the capture of airfields to the north, north-east and north-west of Prague, and it appeared that Student was anxious not only to capture the airfields but to penetrate Prague himself, his object being to prove that airborne forces were capable of carrying out difficult tasks more quickly and efficiently than normal units. Although the operation against Prague proved unnecessary, airborne landings were carried out at Freudenthal, Moravia, on 1 October 1938 in order to test the plan. No parachute drops were involved, but 250 Ju 52s landed on selected rudimentary airstrips and disgorged their troops. Only twelve aircraft were damaged, and the exercise provided much useful experience and knowledge for the future.

At the end of 1938 the command of all parachute and airborne forces was transferred to the *Luftwaffe*; 7 *Fliegerdivision* was confirmed in its status as a full parachute division, while 22 *Infanteriedivision* was to be equipped and trained as an air landing division. Both were to make their mark in the early months of the Second World War.

By 1939, the British were aware that the Germans had been experimenting with the use of airborne forces, and after further investigation it was considered that paratroops might indeed be dropped successfully, although doubts were expressed as to whether the losses incurred in the face of heavy opposition would be warranted by the results likely to be achieved. However, it was felt that something ought to be done. France, Britain's ally, had formed two companies of parachute troops in 1938, with an estimated total strength of 300 men, and the suggestion was that two British officers should visit these units and study their technique. The visit never took place. The arrangements for it, initiated in April 1939, proceeded at such a leisurely pace that they were still incomplete when war was declared, and in October 1939 the visit was cancelled, the French paratroop companies having been disbanded in the meantime.

The subject was not raised again until June 1940, by which time France had been overrun and German troops were in occupation. On 6 June, Prime Minister Winston Churchill wrote a minute for the attention of the War Office. It read:

> *We ought to have a corps of at least 5000 parachute troops, including a proportion of Australians, New Zealanders and Canadians together with some trustworthy people from Norway and France... I hear something is being done to form such a corps but only I believe on a very small scale. Advantage must be taken of the summer to train these troops, who can nonetheless, play their part meanwhile as shock troops in home defence. Pray let me have a note from the War Office on the subject.*

It was a beginning.

CHAPTER FOUR

THE SECOND WORLD WAR

The real testing time for the parachute came during the six years of The Second World War, and it began in the Polish campaign of September 1939. There was no chivalry shown by either side in this bitter three-week battle, and there were frequent reports of shot-down Polish pilots being fired at by enemy fighters as they descended under their parachutes. Take, for example, this account by Second Lieutenant Dzwonek of the 161st Fighter Squadron, flying PZL P.11c fighters in support of the Lodz Army. The squadron did not make contact with the enemy on 1 September, but on the 2nd Dzwonek and Officer Cadet Kremarski shot down a Henschel Hs 126 observation aircraft during a dawn patrol. Encouraged by this success, the same pair took off again at about four o'clock that afternoon to intercept some Heinkel He 111 bombers, but this time they were 'bounced' by Messerschmitt Bf 109s. Kreminski was shot down and killed, and Dzwonek was wounded in his left arm and leg by cannon shells, which also destroyed most of his instrument panel.

Dzwonek was heading back to his base when he saw an air battle in progress between some Polish aircraft and Messerschmitt Bf 110s. He described what happened next.

The Germans were superior in numbers, and I had to decide whether to go to the help of my comrades or land. I soon made up my mind. My left hand was bleeding and useless, so I laid it on my thigh. I also pulled my injured leg out of the way so that I could operate the rudder pedals with my other. I turned away from the fight, climbing over Lodz to gain height, and when I was 500 metres over the battle I put my aircraft into a dive, picking out a Bf 110 and heading towards him at full throttle. I let him have it from close range and pulled up into a climb, turning to attack again, but the 110 broke hard and slipped through my sights. I blacked out briefly as I pulled up into another climb, then as my vision cleared I sighted another 110 and fired a short burst at him. He also broke away.

Dzwonek tried hard to get his sights on other Bf 110s and succeeded in shooting one down, but the air battle was hopelessly one-sided and his own aircraft was hit and set on fire.

Flames reached the cockpit and burned my face. I had to bale out. I began to fry in the cockpit. My struggle with the seat belt and shoulder harness was so long, that I was almost resigned to my fate. Covering my face and eyes against the fire with my left hand, I opened the belts and with a great heave, baled out the port side. We had had instructions to only open our parachute near the ground (after incidents of airmen being strafed in their chutes on 1 September, Polish HQ ordered pilots to open their parachute as low as possible). I looked at my hands – they were white, simply fried, and I thought that 2000 metres lower they might be totally useless. I pulled the handle, and the pain was like holding molten metal. A moment later I felt the jerk – the parachute was open.

I was hanging in the chute at about 2000 metres altitude when I noticed tracers passing near to me. They missed, but this pirate of the Third Reich would not give up and attacked me again. This second time the wave of bullets also spared me. Shells passed to the left and right of my body. The German didn't get a third chance to kill me because my friend Jan Malinowski from 162nd Flight, flying an elderly P.7a, successfully attacked the German. On the first attack he set the right engine of the Bf 110 on fire, and on the second pass killed the pilot. The aircraft fell, crashing in pieces.

During my landing I damaged my backbone. I was transported to the hospital in Pabianice, where I heard someone say I had no chance to see the next sunrise. I did go into a coma for 20 hours. When I awakened, the doctor told me, that in the same hospital was a Bf 110 pilot – the one I downed.

During the Battle of France in May 1940, when the Germans encountered the modern monoplane fighters of the RAF and the French Air Force, many pilots on both sides had remarkable escapes, particularly during the Dunkirk evacuation. Several pilots, their aircraft disabled over the Dunkirk beaches, took to their parachutes only to be killed by small-arms fire as they drifted down, for the troops on the beaches often blazed away indiscriminately at friend and foe alike.

One German pilot who was fortunate to survive was *Oberleutnant* Erich von Oelhaven, whose Junkers Ju 88 dive-bomber was shot down in flames by Spitfires as it was attacking Allied shipping in the English Channel on the morning of 2 June 1940. The pilot held the crippled aircraft steady for long enough to enable his crew to get out, then jumped himself. Bullets crackled around him as he floated down, but miraculously he was unharmed. He drifted in over the beach and landed heavily among the dunes. Slightly winded, he released himself from his parachute and got to his feet to find himself confronted by a group of armed British soldiers. The expressions on their weary, haggard faces left him in no doubt what would happen if he tried to run for it, so he raised his hands.

During the next few hours, von Oelhaven found out what it was like to be on the receiving end of his own side's bombs and shells. Together with the soldiers who had captured him, he cowered in a shallow foxhole in the dunes while geysers of sand and smoke erupted across the beaches. At dusk, urged on by the muzzle of a rifle, he moved with the others down to the water's edge, where a jetty had been built from abandoned army trucks. At its far end was a trawler.

The pilot knew that once he was aboard the ship, one of two fates awaited him: to be sunk by German bombs, or, if he survived, to face a prison cage in England. If he was going to escape it had to be now, in the next couple of minutes, as the queue of battle-stained soldiers shuffled slowly from truck to truck towards the waiting vessel. Cautiously, he looked around; the soldiers nearest to him were almost asleep on their feet.

Gradually, von Oelhaven moved to the edge of the queue. Then, taking a deep breath, he threw himself into the water. He heard a babble of confused shouting, then the sea closed over his head. He groped his way down the line of trucks, squeezed between two of them and broke surface, gasping for air. A couple of feet above him, boards had been laid as a bridge between the two vehicles. Sand filtered through as a steady stream of soldiers tramped across. Sometimes, for long periods of what must have been an hour or more, the queue halted. The pilot could hear the soldiers talking as they waited for the next boat. Then the steady shuffle of feet would begin again.

The hours of darkness seemed endless. The water that lapped around von Oelhaven was red from the fires of Dunkirk and its foul, oily taste made him retch repeatedly. At first the pilot was able to stand upright, his feet touching the bottom, but as the tide came in he was forced to float in order to keep his face above the surface. At high tide his head was jammed in a tiny pocket of air between the water and the planks.

At dawn all movement on the jetty ceased. In the dunes, the last contingents of troops crouched in their holes and prepared to sweat it out under the hot June sun until nightfall, when it would be safe for them to embark. Meanwhile the *Stukas* and the German artillery continued to pound the dwindling bridgehead; time after time, the little jetty shuddered as bombs and shells exploded in the sea, seeking out the small craft that were ferrying soldiers to the larger ships standing offshore. Not daring to move from his hiding place, von Oelhaven was dazed by the concussions that tore through the water.

As the day wore on the pilot became tormented by hunger and thirst. There was a packet of emergency rations in the pocket of his overall, but its protective cover was torn and the contents were a sodden pulp. He tried to force down some of the mess, but his stomach rebelled. His thirst was the worst of all, aggravated by the undrinkable water that was all around him.

Night fell, and the movement of soldiers along the jetty began once more. This time, however, the tramp of feet ceased well before dawn, and von Oelhaven decided to risk moving back along the jetty into shallower water. Worming out of his hiding-place, he waded carefully along the line of trucks until he reached firmer ground. Then he took cover under the planks again. It was an even tighter squeeze than before, but at least he was partly out of the water.

The sun rose on the morning of 4 June. Shelling was still in progress, and von Oelhaven, reasoning that the beaches were still in British hands, decided to stay where he was, at least for the time being. (In fact, the shellfire was directed at French troops, still holding the Dunkirk perimeter.) It was close on ten o'clock when he emerged, into an uncanny silence. The beaches were deserted, except for the piles of equipment left behind by the British. All he wanted now was to get out of the water. He floundered through the shallows and collapsed on the sand. The last thing he remembered, before falling into an exhausted sleep, was the feel of the warm sun on his back. It was there, some time later, that the German soldiers found him. For a third of a million Allied troops, and one German pilot, the nightmare of Dunkirk was over.

The fighting in Belgium and northern France was ended; but for the next three weeks fierce battles went on south of the river Somme, on the ground and in the air. On 3 June the *Luftwaffe* launched Operation Paula, an attack on thirteen airfields in the Paris area, and in the early afternoon seven of the attacking aircraft, Junkers Ju 88s, were intercepted by French fighters as they bombed Etampes aerodrome from 23,000 feet. One of the Ju 88s was shot down, its crew baling out and being taken prisoner. One of them was *Oberst* Josef Kammhuber, who was later to become head of the German night fighter force after being released from his brief French captivity and, after the war, Inspector of the Federal German *Luftwaffe* from 1956 to 1962.

Another German pilot, at that time much more famous than Kammhuber, was also forced to spend a short time in captivity after taking to his parachute. On 5 June, six Dewoitine D.520 fighters – the best in French service – of *Groupe de Chasse* GC I/3 were flying an escort mission in the Brayne-sur-Somme sector, with eight more D.520s of GC II/7 flying top cover. At 25,000 feet over Compiègne the latter were attacked by fifteen Bf 109s; twenty-five more enemy fighters circled watchfully at a distance, ready to pick off any French stragglers. The 109s swept through the French formation in a dive, shooting down two D.520s and badly damaging a third on their first pass. The three pilots of II/7's lower flight turned to meet the attackers head-on and one of them, *Sous-Lieutenant* René Pomier-Layragues, set a 109 on fire with a short burst. Its pilot baled out. He was none other than *Hauptmann* Werner Mölders, commander of III *Gruppe, Jagdgeschwader* 53. At that time his score stood at twenty-five French and British aircraft destroyed.

Taken prisoner by French artillerymen, Mölders at once asked if he might be permitted to meet the man who had shot him down. He was too late. Even as the German ace parachuted down, Pomier-Layragues found himself in a desperate single-handed fight against four 109s. He shot one of them down, but an instant later his D.520 was torn apart by the shells of six more 109s. A ball of fire, it crashed in the suburbs of Marissel and exploded. The pilot had not baled out. Werner Mölders went on to become the first pilot in history to record

Hauptmann Werner Mölders, who was Germany's leading a at the time of the Battle of France, was forced to take to parachute and he spent a brief period in captivity. (Bundesarchiv

The Dewoitine D.520, in which René Pomier-Layragues shot down Werner Mölders, was a match for the Bf 109, but was not available in sufficient numbers. (Author's collection)

100 victories, and added one more to his score before being killed in a flying accident at Breslau in December 1941.

In the spring of 1940, before the German invasion of France and the Low Countries, the Luftwaffe began probing Britain's defences, sending single aircraft from bases in northern Germany to reconnoitre Britain's eastern coastline. Intercepting one such aircraft brought an unexpected consequence for one RAF Spitfire pilot, who baled out in rather unusual circumstances.

On 3 April 1940, Flight Lieutenant Norman Ryder of No 41 Squadron, based at RAF Catterick in North Yorkshire, intercepted a Heinkel He 111 between Redcar and Whitby and shot it down into the sea after a running battle during which his Spitfire was hit in the engine. Ryder sighted a fishing trawler and ditched in the very rough sea about half a mile from it, but he was knocked unconscious by the impact and was some distance below the surface in the rapidly sinking aircraft when he came to. He later recalled:

> *I remember sitting in the cockpit and everything was a bright green. I was very fascinated by the stillness of it all – it was amazing, and I recall watching a lot of bubbles running up the windscreen before my nose and parting as they got to the front. I sat there fascinated by the sight and not a bit afraid. The calm was so restful after the noise. The green colour around me was lovely, but it turned to blackness before I got out. I started to get out by undoing my straps. I stood on my seat and just when I thought I was clear I found my parachute had caught under the sliding hood, and I could not move. I got partially into the cockpit again and at this point noticed that it was getting very much darker as the aircraft sank. I was again nearly hooked up by my parachute, but I wriggled and got clear. By now it was very black and I just saw the silhouette of the tailplane pass my face. I still had on my parachute which hampered my movement, but I managed to dog paddle my way upwards.*

After considerable difficulty, Ryder freed himself from his parachute harness and, completely exhausted by his efforts, was picked up by the trawler crew.

Many shot-down aircrew on both sides owed their lives to the RAF's air-sea rescue craft. Here, an ASR crew practices pulling a pilot aboard. (Richard Derwent)

As time went by, ASR crews became more expert at plucking airmen from the sea quickly. Here, a launch directed by a Westland Lysander travels at speed to rescue a pilot from the English Channel. (Author's collection)

He had the dubious distinction of being the first Spitfire pilot to be shot down by the *Luftwaffe*, a fact compensated for to some extent by the award of the Distinguished Flying Cross.

In August 1940 the Battle of Britain was at its height. Arguably, the most publicised baleout of the battle involved Flight Lieutenant Jame Brindley Nicolson of No 249 Squadron. An Air Ministry News Service Bulletin, issued three months later, told at least most of the story.

> *The Victoria Cross, which has been awarded to Flight Lieutenant J.B. Nicolson (A.M. Bulletin No.2255), is the first V.C. to be won by a fighter pilot since the war began.*
>
> *He has gained his V.C. for refusing to jump from a blazing Hurricane until he had destroyed his enemy although it was his first fight and he had been twice wounded. For forty-eight hours doctors fought for his life but now he has almost completely recovered.*
>
> *Flight Lieutenant Nicolson, who is 23, was on patrol near the Southampton area with his squadron on the early afternoon of 16 August. He saw three Junkers 88 bombers crossing the bows of the squadron about 4 miles away, and he was detailed to chase a Junkers with his section.*
>
> *He got within a mile of them, and then he saw a squadron of Spitfires attack and shoot them down, so he turned back to join his squadron, climbing from 15,000 to 18,000 feet.*
>
> *Suddenly, as he himself said, there were four big bangs inside his*

aircraft. They were cannon shells from a Messerschmitt 110. One tore through the hood and sent splinters to his left eye. The second cannon shell struck his spare petrol tank which exploded, and set the machine on fire. The third shell crashed into the cockpit and tore away his trouser leg. The fourth hit his left boot and wounded his heel.

As Flight Lieutenant Nicolson turned to avoid further shots into his burning aeroplane, he suddenly found that the Me110 had overtaken him and was right in his gunsight. His dashboard was shattered and was, in his own words, 'Dripping like treacle' with the heat. The Messerschmitt was two hundred yards in front and both were diving at about 400 m.p.h.

As Flight Lieutenant Nicolson pressed the gun button he could see his right thumb blistering in the heat. He could also see his left hand, which was holding the throttle open, blistering in the flames.

The Messerschmitt zig-zagged this way and that trying to avoid the hail of fire from the blazing Hurricane. By this time the heat was so great that Nicolson had to put his feet on the seat beneath his parachute. He continued the flight for several minutes until the Messerschmitt disappeared in a steep dive. Eyewitnesses later reported that they had seen it crash a few miles out to sea.

On losing sight of the enemy, Nicolson attempted to jump out, but struck his head on the hood above him. He immediately threw back the hood and tried to jump again. Then he realised he had not undone the strap holding him in the cockpit. One of these straps broke. He undid the other, and at last succeeded in jumping out.

He dived head first, and after several somersaults in the air pulled the rip-cord with considerable difficulty. It took him something like 20 minutes to reach the ground.

A Messerschmitt came screaming past, and as he floated down, he pretended that he was dead. When the Me. had gone he noticed for the first time that his left heel had been struck. Blood was oozing out of the lace holes in his boots. He tried to see what other injuries he had received and found that he was able to move all his limbs.

At one moment as he was coming down, he thought he would hit a high tension cable but managed to manoeuvre in the sky so that he missed it. Reaching the ground, he saw a cyclist and managed to land in a field near to him. When help came Flight Lieutenant Nicolson immediately dictated a telegram to his wife in Yorkshire to say that he had been shot down but was safe.

He looked at his watch, and found it still ticking though the glass had melted and the strap had burned to a thread.

'When I saw the Messerschmitt in front of me I remember shouting out, "I'll teach you some manners you Hun", he said later, "I am glad I got him, though perhaps pilots who have had more experience of air fighting would have done the wise thing and baled out immediately the *aircraft caught fire. I did not think of anything at the time but to shoot him down."*

'*Curiously enough, although the heat inside must have been intense, in the excitement I did not feel much pain. In fact, I remember watching the skin being burnt off my left hand. All I was concerned about was keeping the throttle open to get my first Hun. I must confess that I felt all in as I came down. I confess too that I thought I might faint, but I did not lose consciousness at all. Thinking of the shock I know follows severe burning I asked the doctors who examined me to give me a shot of morphine just in case.*'

The bulletin does not tell the whole of the story. As Nicolson approached the ground, a Home Guard sergeant, mistaking him for a German, opened fire on him with a shotgun, the pellets hitting the already wounded pilot in the side. The cyclist, a well-built butcher's boy, was so outraged that he beat up the sergeant, who was taken off to hospital in an ambulance intended for Nicolson!

Nicolson later returned to flying duties and, promoted to wing commander, was posted to the Far East. On 2 May 1945, he was killed when a Consolidated Liberator of No 355 Squadron, in which he was flying as an observer, crashed into the sea 130 miles south of Calcutta as the result of an engine fire.

The Hawker Hurricane, one of which Nicolson was flying on the day he earned the VC, could absorb an extraordinary amount of battle damage, as this photograph shows. (British Aerospace)

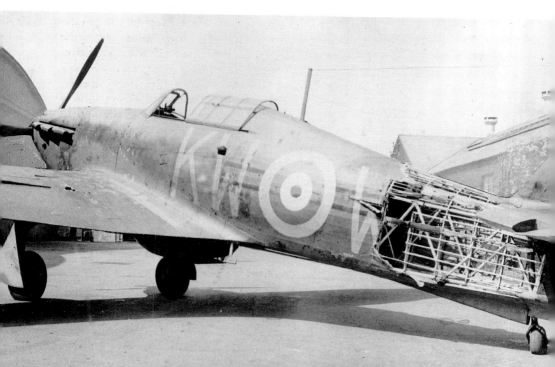

The Hurricane's cockpit. If fuel tanks were hit and set on fire, pilots had a maximum of eleven seconds to get out. (British Aerospace)

Nicolson's VC was awarded for an action carried out, literally, in the heat of the moment, but others, which also involved aircrew baling out, were awarded for acts of cool, premeditated gallantry. One such was Squadron Leader Leonard Trent, a 28-year-old New Zealander serving with No 487 (RNZAF) Squadron. During that month both RAF Bomber Command and the US Eighth Army Air Force carried out a series of intensive attacks on power stations in Holland, which were supplying energy to the German war effort. All these missions were flown in daylight, and the cost in aircraft and crews was high.

On 3 May, eleven Lockheed Venturas of No 487 Squadron, led by Len Trent, took off from their base at Methwold in Norfolk to attack the main power station in Amsterdam. Apart from disrupting the power supply to German-controlled industries in the area, the raid was designed to encourage Dutch workers in their resistance to enemy pressure. The importance of bombing the target, which was heavily defended, was strongly impressed on the crews taking part in the operation, and before take-off Trent told his deputy that he intended to go in whatever happened.

Everything went well until the eleven Venturas and their fighter escort were

Hawker Hurricanes of No 601 Squadron in the kind of formation used by the RAF during the Battle of Britain. Pilots concentrated more on keeping an eye on adjacent aircraft instead of looking out for the enemy. (IWM)

A Lockheed Ventura bomber of the type flown by Leonard Trent on the day he won the VC. (Lockheed)

over the Dutch coast, when one of the bombers was hit by flak and had to turn back. A minute later large numbers of enemy fighters appeared; these engaged the Spitfire escort, which soon lost touch with the Venturas. The latter closed up tightly for mutual protection and started their run towards the target, expecting to rendezvous with more friendly fighters over Amsterdam, but the fighters had arrived in the target area much too soon and had been recalled.

Within moments the Venturas were being savagely attacked by twenty Messerschmitts and Focke-Wulfs. One after the other, six of the bombers went down in flames in the space of four minutes. The remaining four, with Trent at their head, continued doggedly towards the target. The dwindling formation now ran into murderous anti-aircraft fire, which accounted for two more Venturas. Trent and the other surviving crew made accurate bombing runs, harassed all the time by enemy fighters that braved their own flak to press home their attacks. Trent got in a lucky burst with his nose gun at a Focke-Wulf 190, which flicked into a spin and crashed. A moment later the other Ventura received a direct hit and exploded. Trent turned away from the target area, but his aircraft too was hit and began to break up. Trent and his navigator were thrown clear, descending under their parachutes to become prisoners of war; the other two crew members were killed. After the war, when the full story of the raid emerged, Trent was awarded the Victoria Cross. Later, as a wing commander, Trent commanded one of the first RAF V-bomber squadrons, No 214, which was equipped with Vickers Valiants at Marham in Norfolk. He retired with the rank of group captain.

A low-level attack by RAF bombers against a target in Holland.
(Author's collection)

On the night of 26/27 April, 1944, 226 aircraft of RAF Bomber Command were despatched to attack Schweinfurt, the scene of some of the bloodiest encounters of the air war in 1943 between the *Luftwaffe* and the US Eighth Army Air Force. As the Americans knew to their cost, Schweinfurt, the centre of the German ball-bearing industry, was heavily defended by flak. For night defence there was a vast array of searchlights and smokescreens. The five big ball-bearing factories in the town had been severely damaged by the USAAF, but intelligence sources indicated that their production was beginning to pick up rapidly and it was clear that another major attack was necessary.

The bomber force made a lengthy detour across southern France to confuse the enemy defences, but the ruse did not succeed and the night fighters were waiting. The wind also veered and strengthened, delaying the main marker and flare force, which meant that there was a considerable interval between the arrival of the initial markers and the main markers. As a result many of the main force aircraft had to orbit in the target area, waiting until the aiming point was clearly marked.

Many of the bombers engaged in the Schweinfurt mission were heavily attacked by fighters as they were leaving the target area. One of them, an Avro Lancaster of No 106 Squadron, was climbing away when it was intercepted by a Focke-Wulf Fw 190 at 20,000 feet. The captain took violent evasive action, but the enemy aircraft scored many hits and a fire broke out near a fuel tank on the upper surface of the starboard wing, between the fuselage and inner engine.

Although wounded by shell splinters in his right leg and shoulder, the flight engineer, Sergeant Norman Jackson, volunteered to try to put out the fire. Pushing a hand-held fire extinguisher into the top of his lifejacket and clipping on a parachute pack, Jackson climbed on to the navigation table and deliberately opened his parachute inside the aircraft, while Flying Officer Higgins (navigator) and Flight Sergeant Toft (bomb aimer) sorted out the rigging lines and parachute to prepare themselves as 'anchor-men'. Releasing the upper escape hatch, Jackson squeezed himself out into the freezing 200 mph slipstream. Firmly grasping the edge of the open hatch he edged his body out, lay flat along the top of the fuselage and lowered himself until his feet met the wing root below. He flung himself forward and managed to grasp the leading edge air intake and directed the contents of the extinguisher into an engine cowling opening. The flames died down momentarily. The Lancaster banked to port, taking evasive action against the returning German fighter which raked the aircraft with cannon

Norman Jackson, VC.

fire again and wounded Jackson for the second time. After the impact of the shellfire, the extinguisher was blown away. The fire once again erupted, and soon searing flames were licking at Jackson's face, hands and clothing. It was not long before the intense pain compelled him to let go; he was swept through the flames and over the trailing edge of the wing, dragging his parachute behind.

When the other crew members last saw Jackson's parachute, its canopy was only partly inflated and it was burning in several places. It seemed as though there was little hope for the flight engineer's survival. By this time the fire was raging uncontrollably across most of the wing, and the pilot ordered the others to abandon the aircraft. Four of them, including Higgins and Toft, survived; the pilot, Flying Officer Mifflen, and Flight Sergeant Johnson, the rear gunner, were killed.

Norman Jackson, however, was still very much alive, although in a pitiable condition. Unable to control his descent because of his severely burnt hands, he landed heavily, sustaining a broken ankle. At daybreak, in great pain from

An Avro Lancaster over Normandy, 1944. (Author's collection)

his ankle, burns and the wounds he had sustained earlier, he managed to crawl to a nearby village, where he was taken prisoner. Jackson spent about ten months in hospital at Obermassfeld, slowly recuperating from his injuries, before being transferred to *Stalag* Kc at Bad Suiza, Mulhausen. He made two escapes from the prison camp, and on the second attempt succeeded in contacting U.S. troops from Patton's Third Army near Munich. Norman Jackson was returned to Britain on V.E. Day and was gazetted for the award of the Victoria Cross on 26 October, 1945.

The intensive air operations in support of the Normandy landings in June 1944 brought the award of the Victoria Cross to yet another member of RAF Bomber Command. It happened on the night of 12/13 June, when Lancasters of No 419 Squadron, Royal Canadian Air Force – operating out of RAF Middleton St George in County Durham – were engaged in an attack on marshalling yards at Cambrai. Shortly after midnight Flying Officer G.P.

Brophy, the rear gunner of Lancaster A-Able, warned his captain, Flying officer Art Debreyne, that a Junkers Ju 88 was approaching from behind and below. The Lancaster was just beginning an evasive corkscrew manoeuvre when the port wing and aft section of the fuselage were hit by cannon shells. Fire broke out immediately between the mid-upper and rear gun turrets.

Debrayne ordered his crew to bale out and managed to retain partial control while the forward crew members were leaving via the front hatch. Having remained at the controls for what he considered a long enough period to allow the others to get out, the pilot also jumped at a height of 1300 feet.

Unknown to the captain, however – the intercom was dead – Brophy was still in the rear turret. As there was no longer hydraulic power to rotate the turret, he had to turn it by hand far enough to permit him to reach his parachute. Having obtained it he began to turn the turret beamwards, intending to bale out directly from his

Andrew Charles Mynarski, VC.

position, but the rotation gear handle came away in his hand and he found himself hopelessly trapped.

Meanwhile, the mid-upper gunner, Pilot Officer Andrew Mynarski, had recognised Brophy's plight while on his way to the rear escape hatch. He unhesitatingly made his way through the flames to try to release him, and as he did so his parachute and clothing caught fire. All his efforts to free Brophy were in vain, and in the short time left it was impossible to do more. Brophy realised this and waved Mynarski away, indicating that he should try to save is own life.

Mynarski fought his way back through the flames to the escape hatch. There he paused, turned – and as a last gesture to his trapped friend – stood to attention in his burning flying clothing and saluted before jumping. On the ground, Frenchmen watched as he descended like a blazing torch, his parachute and clothing aflame. When they reached him he was beyond all help, and died of severe burns shortly afterwards.

Miraculously, the only man who had witnessed Mynarski's courage lived to tell the story. The Lancaster struck the ground in a flat attitude and skidded along for a considerable distance. The vibration freed the rear turret and Brophy was thrown clear. He was knocked out for a while, but regained consciousness to find that he had not suffered serious injury. He succeeded in contacting the French Resistance and returned to England early in September. He at once made the facts of Mynarski's heroism known to the authorities, testifying that his colleague could almost certainly have left the aircraft safely had he not paused to try to effect the rescue. Mynarski must have been fully aware that in trying to free the rear gunner he was sacrificing his own life, but he seemed unaffected by any instinct of self-preservation. On 11 October, 1946, Pilot Officer Andrew Charles Mynarski was posthumously awarded the Victoria Cross. [Author's note: As this was being written, plans were well advanced to erect a statue to Andrew Mynarksi VC at Durham Tees Valley Airport – the former RAF Middleton St George. The plan was initiated by the region's local newspaper, the *Northern Echo*, which launched an appeal for public donations].

It was desperately unfortunate that Mynarski should lose his life, while the fellow crew member he had given up for lost was in fact spared. But other aircrew during the Second World War were also spared in extraordinary circumstances.

* * * *

The cockpit was like an icebox. Commander Sergei Kurzenkov had been flying north-westwards into the freezing darkness deep inside the Arctic Circle for forty-five minutes since leaving snow-covered Vaenga airfield, near Murmansk, on the north-west tip of Russia, and his body was numb from the bitter cold that cut through his fur-lined flying suit. He shook his head to clear away the drowsiness brought on by the cold and the monotonous roar of the engine, knowing that he had to stay alert at all costs. The lives of thousands depended on his mission.

It was February, 1943, and Russia was at bay, although there were signs that the tide was turning. The German Sixth Army, trapped and surrounded at Stalingrad, had just surrendered. Everything would depend on the crucial offensives that both sides were planning once the spring thaw had come and gone.

For the past year, a steady flow of war materials from Britain and the United States had been reaching the Soviet Union via the Arctic sea route. The Allied convoys had suffered terrible losses in attacks by German U-boats, aircraft and surface warships during 1942, and now the Germans were standing ready to fall on another such convoy, heading for the Kola Inlet. They had amassed all available bombers of the Norway-based Air Fleet 5 at Kirkenes, on the northern tip of Norway, and were determined to destroy the convoy. The Russians were equally as determined to stop them.

Kurzenkov, who was flying an Ilyushin Il-2 ground attack aircraft, was preceding a strong force of Soviet bombers, its target Kirkenes. His job was to attack the airfield first, starting fires which would lead the bombers to their objective. It was no easy task; from 12,000 feet he could see no landmarks on the snow-covered ground. There was no moon, and the landscape was just a dull, grey blur, broken here and there by the darker shadows of wooded hillsides.

Suddenly, he caught a brief flicker of light in the darkness ahead. A few seconds later he saw it again, and this time there was no mistaking the

An Ilyushin Il-2 ground attack aircraft, which Commander Kurzenkov was flying at the time of his amazing escape. (Author's collection)

navigation lights of an aircraft, flashing on an off. The cold suddenly forgotten, Kurzenkov peered into the night. A moment later he found what he was looking for: the glow of a flarepath, its light carefully masked. He put the Il-2 into a shallow dive towards the objective, and found to his satisfaction that, as he narrowed the distance, he was able to pick out the dark shapes of bombers parked on the snow alongside the runway. A searchlight flicked on, almost immediately catching the Russian aircraft in its beam and blinding the pilot. Flak began to burst around the Ilyushin and Kurzenkov felt the machine shudder as splinters ripped into it. Then he was over the airfield, the parked bombers squarely in his sights. He pulled the bomb release toggle and turned away steeply from the glare of the searchlights. Looking back, he saw his bombs explode among a group of Junkers 88s, setting several of them on fire.

A sudden, fierce glare enveloped him as an anti-aircraft shell burst over the port wing. The cockpit canopy flew off with a bang and the instrument panel, pulverised by splinters, fell across his knees in a mass of shattered dials. More splinters seared into Kurzenkov's legs and for a moment the pain was so excruciating that he almost blacked out, but the icy blast of air rushing into the cockpit lashed at his face and revived him. He opened the throttle and put the aircraft into a steep climb, desperate to get away from the extremely accurate flak that continued to explode around him. There was another violent thud as another shell found its mark, and this time a dull red glow appeared in the port wing, turning rapidly into a long streamer of brilliant flame.

Its wings and fuselage gashed by shell splinters, the aircraft climbed sluggishly to 11,000 feet. Fighting the pain in his legs, Kurzenkov levelled out and called his base. Miraculously, the radio was still working. The controller at Vaenga replied almost immediately and gave him a course to steer for home.

The pilot needed all his failing strength to keep the shattered aircraft steady. He saw the flames creeping steadily along the wing towards the cockpit and knew that in a matter of minutes he would be roasted alive in the explosion of the aircraft's fuel tanks. The seconds ticked by with agonising slowness. The whole wing was a mass of fire now, and hungry flames were already licking into the cockpit. Kurzenkov tried to shield his eyes from the searing heat with one hand, but it was an effort to hold it up to his face. By this time he was seriously weakened by loss of blood.

Finally, he could bear the heat no longer. Not caring whether he was over Russian territory or not, he undid his seat harness with scorched fingers and tried to claw his way out of the cockpit. Several times he tried to drag himself over the side, but each time the rushing airflow forced his weakened body back into his seat. Panic gripped him, and at that moment his mind became crystal clear. Using what was left of his strength, he shoved the control column hard over. The aircraft rolled over on its back and Kurzenkov fell out of the open cockpit, away from the blistering heat into a withering blast of icy air and a temperature of thirty degrees below zero. He let himself fall, knowing that if he opened his parachute at this height he would probably freeze to death before he reached the ground. He counted off the seconds slowly. Then when he judged that he had fallen five or six thousand feet, he pulled the ripcord.

It came away in his hand.

Frantically, he groped behind him, searching for his parachute pack. It was not there. The harness had been severed by shell splinters. Another inch or so, and they would have severed his spine.

It didn't matter. He was going to die, anyway. Strangely, he felt no fear. His last thought before he blacked out was that it was better to go this way than burn to death.

As a matter of fact, death wasn't at all unpleasant; rather like drifting on a white cloud, with no feeling at all. Then Kurzenkov tasted blood in his mouth, and realised he was still alive. He was lying in snowdrift at the foot of a steep slope. He gave a crazy laugh and tried to jump to his feet, only to collapse, gasping with the pain in his legs. He lay still, trying to assemble his scattered thoughts. He had no idea where he was, but one thing he knew for certain: he was not going to be captured by the Germans; he still had his revolver at his belt, and he would use it.

Then he heard something, a dull rumble that swelled into a roar. He recognised the sound of Russian aero-engines, quite different from the throb of German motors. Vaenga airfield must be just over the hill. The pilot wept with misery and frustration as he suddenly realised that he was going to die helplessly, like a wounded animal in a trap, almost within sight of home.

He lay there in the snow, bouts of consciousness and pain alternating with periods of merciful oblivion. Then, as he was emerging from a period of darkness into the grey, pain-filled world of awareness, he heard Russian voices. Dragging his pistol from its holster, he fired a couple of shots. The voices grew louder and he fired again. His last memory before losing consciousness was of a circle of white faces peering down at him, and of a Russian infantryman wrapping his injured legs in an army greatcoat.

After a long spell in hospital, Sergei Kurzenkov returned to flying duties. Flying with various fighter units, he went on to destroy twelve enemy aircraft and was awarded the gold star of a Hero of the Soviet Union, Russia's highest decoration. He retired from the Soviet Air Force in 1950.

Kurzenkov was lucky to survive, but others have been even luckier. On notable survivor was another Soviet airman, Lieutenant Ivan M. Chisov, who was the pilot of an Ilyushin Il-4 twin-engined heavy bomber when it was attacked by a dozen Messerschmitt Bf 109s in January 1942 and heavily damaged. Chisov baled out at 22,000 feet, together with the surviving members of his crew, and because of the presence of the enemy fighters he decided to delay opening his parachute until he was closer to the ground. The problem was that he lost consciousness on the way down and woke up lying in snow at the bottom of a steep ravine. Apart from some cuts and bruises, he had some compressed vertebrae and a fractured pelvis. He also returned to flying duties and survived the war.

A Boeing B-17G Flying Fortress. The under-fuselage ball turret, from which Alan Magee was thrown, is just visible behind the trailing edge of the wing. (Author's collection)

A formation of B-17 Flying Fortresses over Germany. The number of occasions when a crew had to bale out when their aircraft was hit by bombs falling from higher up is not recorded. (Author's collection)

Another airman who had more than his share of luck was Staff Sergeant Alan Magee, a ball turret gunner on a B-17 Flying Fortress of the 360th Squadron, 303rd Bomb Group, US Eighth Air Force, which took off from Molesworth, Northamptonshire, on 3 January 1943 to attack a torpedo storage depot at St Nazaire, on the French Atlantic coast. The bomber was hit by enemy fighters over the target and exploded before Magee had a chance to put on his parachute. Hurled out into the freezing air at 20,000 feet, he lost consciousness and woke up in a first aid station, having fallen through the glass roof of St Nazaire railway station. Magee sustained multiple injuries, including a severely damaged arm, which was saved by a German doctor. Two other crew members also escaped with their lives. Lieutenant G.M. Herrington, the navigator, lost his leg to enemy gunfire, but survived the descent to be taken prisoner and later repatriated; he died in 1987. Staff Sergeant J.I. Gordon also baled out and was taken prisoner.

On 23 September, 1995, Alan Magee, accompanied by his wife, Helen, returned to St Nazaire to take part in a ceremony sponsored by French citizens, dedicating a memorial to his seven fellow crew members who were killed when the B-17 crashed in the forest of La Baule Escoublac. The Magees were welcomed to France by Michel Lugez, American Memorial Association President, who greeted them at the Nantes/Atlantique Airport and acted as their escort throughout the various ceremonies. On Saturday morning, 3 September, after a mass in memory of the seven dead airmen, the entourage proceeded to the crash site where the memorial was unveiled and dedicated; it was also decorated with many wreaths. This was followed by the planting of a 'Tree of Peace' by Magee. During his visit to St. Nazaire, Alan visited the Hermitage Hotel, where he was treated by the German doctor, and also the submarine pens, the harbour, and the railway station where the glass roof had broken his fall fifty years before. As he had been unconscious at the time of the impact, it was the first time he had ever set eyes on it. Alan Magee died in 2003 at the age of 84.

One of the best known 'free fall' stories concerns Flight Sergeant Nicholas Alkemade, a Royal Air Force rear gunner. On the night of 24/25 March, 1944, Alkemade was part of the crew of a No 115 Squadron Lancaster which set out to attack Berlin. The raid was a big one, with over 800 aircraft despatched, but the attacking force met with unexpectedly strong and unforecast winds and became widely scattered, 72 aircraft being lost to radar-predicted flak and night fighters.

It was a night fighter that accounted for Alkemade's Lancaster, which was heavily damaged and set ablaze. The skipper gave the order to bale out.

I found myself in a ring of fire that was singeing my face and melting the rubber of my oxygen mask, Alkemade said later. I leaned back, pushed open the turret doors, and reached into the fuselage to grab my parachute from its rack. The whole length of the fuselage was blazing. The flames reached right down to the door of my turret. And there, in a fierce little fire of its own, my parachute was blazing, too.

For a brief moment I stared while it dissolved before my eyes. It was not so much a feeling of fear, or dismay, or horror, as a sensation, a sort of twisting in the stomach. As I turned back I noticed that my leather trousers and jacket had caught fire. The turret was like an inferno, and getting worse all the time. My face was tingling, and I could almost feel my flesh shrivelling in that unbearable heat.

Desperately, seeking to escape from the heat, I rotated the turret to port, elbowed the sliding doors open, and back-flipped out into space, 18,000 feet deep. As I left the Lancaster I half sensed, half saw, a great explosion from her, then I was falling through the cold night air. I found myself dropping to attention, as though it were a formal occasion, and beyond my feet I had an impression of stars shining. I felt quite calm as the air swept past me, faster and faster, until it became difficult to breathe. 'Funny,' I thought, 'but if this is dying, it's not at all strange.' Then the rushing air, the stars, the ground, the sky, all merged and were forgotten as unconsciousness crept over me...

I opened my eyes to see the stars shining through a dark lattice of pine branches. It was peaceful, and rather lovely. I don't remember feeling surprised about the fact that I was alive; it was not until ages later that realisation came to me and I began to sweat. I looked at my watch and found it read 3.25. I had jumped shortly after midnight, so I must have been unconscious for more than three hours.

I wriggled my toes. They worked. Then I moved my arms, legs and neck. Everything seemed to work, though my right knee was a little stiff. Then I rolled over, and noticed for the first time that I was lying in a small drift of snow, about eighteen inches deep. Later, I realised that I owed my life to the pine branches and the snow, both of which had helped to break my fall. I was very sore and the cold was beginning to creep through my limbs. As I couldn't walk and would only freeze or starve where I lay, I pulled up the whistle hanging from my jacket and blew a series of blasts. After that I lay still, alternately blowing my whistle and smoking a cigarette, until a German search party found me.

Alkemade's principal problem now was that his German interrogators, who visited him hospital while he was having twigs and bits of perspex removed from his flesh, flatly refused to believe his story. It was only when they discovered his parachute harness, with no canopy attached to it, and located the wreck of the Lancaster with the charred remnants of his parachute still inside, that they accepted the facts. Alkemade spent the rest of the war in a PoW camp near Frankfurt. He died on 22 June, 1987.

Alkemade, and others who survived long drops without a parachute, undoubtedly owed their survival at least in part because they lost consciousness during the fall and their bodies were consequently in a relaxed state at the time of the impact.

* * * *

Like Nicholas Alkemade, Australian Flight Lieutenant Joe Herman made a precipitate exit from a bomber minus his parachute. He survived because he was, quite literally, in the right place at the right time.

Herman was the captain of a Halifax of No 466 Squadron, Royal Australian Air Force, which took off from Driffield in Yorkshire on the night of 4 November 1944 to attack Bochum in the Ruhr. It was not an easy trip to the target area; on two occasions the aircraft was coned by searchlights and subjected to heavy flak. Feeling uneasy, Herman ordered his crew to clip on their parachutes, although for the time being he was too busy taking evasive action to bother about his own.

The target was successfully bombed and Herman turned on a course for home, starting a descent from 18,000 to 10,000 feet. At that moment, the Halifax was hit by flak three times in rapid succession, once in the fuselage just behind the wing main spar and twice in the wings. Both wing tanks were ruptured, and within seconds the whole wing was ablaze. Without hesitation, knowing that the aircraft was likely to explode at any moment, Herman gave the order to bale out.

In the mid-upper turret, the gunner, Flight Sergeant John 'Irish' Vivash, had been wounded in the leg by a flak splinter. On hearing Herman's order he wormed his way painfully out of his turret and started to crawl towards the forward escape hatch, noticing Herman leave the pilot's seat to retrieve his own parachute, stowed in the flight engineer's crew station. At that moment the Halifax's starboard wing folded back with a blinding flash of burning petrol and the bomber flicked onto its back and then began to spin down.

The explosion of the wing root was the last Vivash remembered; his next recollection was feeling a draught of cold air on his face and a not unpleasant sensation of falling. He had no recollection of operating his ripcord, yet above his head the silken canopy was fully deployed, swinging him in long gentle arcs through the air. Suddenly the pendulum-like swinging motion stopped and he realised he was falling straight down, still supported by his parachute, but with something that felt like a dead weight pulling on his legs. Reaching down with an exploratory hand, his fingers made contact with what felt like someone else's body.

Vivash later recalled his exact, rather incongruous, words.

'Is anyone else around here?' he asked.

'Yes, me,' a voice answered, 'I'm here, hanging on to you'.

'Is that you, Joe?' queried Vivash.

'Yes, but I haven't got a 'chute, Irish. I seem to have bumped into you on my way down.'

Both Herman and Vivash realised that they had been blown clear of the aircraft, the pilot without his parachute. Falling from 17,000 feet, resigned to the fact that he was going to die, Herman had suddenly bumped into something solid and instinctively wrapped his arms around it. The 'something' was Vivash's legs, outstretched as the gunner reached the top of one of his swings. Herman clung on for dear life as the two descended under a single parachute.

A few minutes later Herman, glancing down, saw some tree-tops rushing towards him and just had time to yell a warning before he hit the ground with a thump that knocked the wind out of him. Herman landed directly on top of him, breaking two of his ribs. It was a small price to pay for his life. Both men were captured after four days of evading the enemy, surviving their captivity to return to Australia.

* * * *

Wartime, with all its pressures and demands to rush new types of combat aircraft into service as quickly as possible, was a difficult and dangerous time for test pilots. Messerschmitt's Chief Test Pilot Fritz Wendel had to test some quite dreadful aircraft types during his career, including the Messerschmitt Me 210.

'I was never happy about the Me 210,' he said later. 'I have only been forced to bale out of an aircraft twice, and the first time was from this twin-engined fighter-bomber, Wendel described his first flight in the Me 210:

It was on 5 September, 1940, that I took off from Augsburg-Haunstetten in the Me 210V-2. We had more than a suspicion that the tail assembly was weak, and that there was a strong possibility that it would part company with the rest of the airframe in a dive. I was flying solo, the mechanic who usually occupied the radio operator's seat on test flights being left on the ground as this flight was likely to be more than usually dangerous.

During the climb I recall the thought flashing through my mind: 'If something goes wrong, remember to avoid baling out over the forest.' At 9000 feet I checked my instruments and started the planned series of dives, my unpleasant thoughts temporarily forgotten. Stick forward... down went the nose and the needle began to creep round the airspeed indicator. Stick back, and the nose lifted. Stick forward... back... forward, and so on. One more shallow dive and back to the airfield. A thousand feet showed on the altimeter and I began to level off. Then it happened, and right over that blasted Siebentischwald again! The plane shuddered, the tail fluttered, and bang, the starboard elevator broke off! Immediately the plane went into a half-loop downwards. Before I could gather my wits I was flying on my back in the direction from which I had just come. I knew exactly what would happen now, as I had seen the same thing happen to the fist prototype some weeks before. The plane would fly inverted for several seconds and then dive straight into the ground.

Hanging on my seat straps, head downwards, I automatically grabbed the release pin, but I hadn't jettisoned the canopy. In that split second I fumbled for the roof's emergency release lever, pulled it, and the canopy flew off with a bang. I pulled the release pin. ...the chute opened with a glorious crack. I looked down, and there were those damned trees almost

The Messerschmitt Me 210 gave German test pilot Fritz Wendel some very unpleasant moments. (Author's collection)

touching my feet. But I was in luck, for the wind blew me towards the only clearing that I could see, and I escaped with nothing worse than a sprained ankle. I had lost a prototype, but at least I had proved its unsatisfactory characteristics and had lived to tell the tale. But there are few things in the world harder than proving to an aircraft designer that his latest pet creation in simply not good enough.

Wendel's second baleout happened on 14 April 1944. The aircraft involved was a Messerschmitt Bf 109H, a high-altitude fighter-reconnaissance version of the Bf 109 with a longer wing span. A small number of these aircraft was delivered to 3 (F) 121, based at Guyancourt near Paris, and Wendel went there to investigate complaints by the pilots that they were experiencing wing flutter in dives. The test pilot went back to Augsburg and began extensive tests on the Bf 109H, which was capable of reaching an altitude of 47,000 feet.

On 14 April I took off in an aircraft of this type, climbed to 16,000 feet, and put the plane into a shallow dive. Soon the needle of the airspeed indicator was flickering on the 500mph mark, but at 10,500 feet the wings began to flutter. Carefully I eased the stick back, but with a hell of a bang the port wing flew off and the plane whipped into a tight circle. I released the canopy and seat straps, but the centrifugal force was holding me against the port side of the cockpit. I finally succeeded in pulling myself out of the crippled plane and delayed pulling my ripcord in an attempt to put as much distance between myself and the spiralling aircraft before the chute opened.

Dropping like a stone, I suddenly remembered that I had forgotten to adjust my parachute straps before take-off. I forced my hand up to my left shoulder to feel for my shoulder strap. It wasn't there. In the seconds in which I made this frightening discovery I had never been so scared before in my life. Then, to my intense relief, I found that the loose straps had only slipped down to my elbows. My joy when that glorious white blossom flowered out above me is indescribable.

I now had a chance to look around to see what had happened to my plane. Far below I could see a Flak emplacement with its personnel scurrying for slit trenches in their haste to take cover from the falling wreckage. There was the fuselage plummeting down, now without its engine, but that damned port wing was sailing through the air straight in my direction. I shut my eyes, expecting the wing to cut through me or the parachute shrouds like a giant knife. One second, two seconds... still nothing. I opened my eyes just in time to see the giant knife swish past my feet! When I had disentangled myself from the chute, the troops for the Flak emplacement told me the incredible fact that the fuselage had hit the ground first, then the port wing, and finally the engine. Presumably the prop had still been turning and had lowered the engine like a helicopter.

* * * *

Of all the tasks men have to perform in war, one of the least enviable is parachuting into the arms of the enemy; but that is what paratroops are paid to do. No less gallant are the crews of the transport aircraft who must fly straight and level, often through withering fire, until the paratroops have made their exit, and then return to the cauldron to drop badly-needed supplies. On particular act of gallantry at Arnhem in September 1944 speaks for all of them.

The resupply mission of Tuesday, 19 September 1944, resulted in the award of RAF Transport Command's only Victoria Cross. Its recipient was Flight Lieutenant David Lord, DFC, of No 271 Squadron, which was equipped with Dakotas. The citation reads:

Flight Lieutenat Lord was pilot and captain of a Dakota aircraft detailed to drop supplies at Arnhem on the afternoon of the 19th September 1944. Our airborne troops had been surrounded and were being pressed into a small area defended by a large number of anti-aircraft guns. Aircrews were warned that intense opposition would be met over the dropping zone. To ensure accuracy they were ordered to fly at 900 feet when dropping their containers.

While flying at 1500 feet near Arnhem the starboard wing of Flight Lieutenant Lord's aircraft was twice hit by anti-aircraft fire. The starboard engine was set on fire. He would have been justified in leaving the main stream of supply aircraft and continuing at the same height or even abandoning his aircraft. But on learning that his crew were uninjured and that the dropping zone would be reached in three minutes he said he would complete his mission, as the troops were in dire need of supplies.

By now the starboard engine was burning furiously. Flight Lieutenant Lord came down to 900 feet, where he was singled out for concentrated fire from all the anti-aircraft guns. On reaching the dropping zone he kept the aircraft on a straight and level course while supplies were dropped. At the end of the run, he was told that two containers remained.

Although he must have known that the collapse of the starboard wing could not be long delayed, Flight Lieutenant Lord circled, rejoined the stream of aircraft and made a second run to drop the remaining supplies. These manoeuvres took eight minutes in all, the aircraft being continuously under heavy anti-aircraft fire.

His task completed, Flight Lieutenant Lord ordered his crew to abandon the Dakota, making no attempt himself to leave the aircraft, which was down to 500 feet. A few seconds later the starboard wing collapsed and the aircraft fell in flames. There was only one survivor, who was flung out while assisting other members of the crew to put on their parachutes.

By continuing his mission in a damaged and burning aircraft, descending to drop the supplies accurately, returning to the dropping zone a second time and, finally, remaining at the controls to give is crew a chance of escape, Flight Lieutenant Lord displayed supreme valour and self-sacrifice.

British paratroops check their kit before boarding their aircraft bound for Arnhem. The aircraft in this case are Short Stirlings of No 620 Squadron. (Author's collection)

The sole survivor was Flight Lieutenant Harry King, the navigator, who had been helping the Army dispatchers to push the supply panniers overboard. As soon as Lord gave the order to bale out, King began to help the dispatchers with their parachute harness, hoping that there was still enough height for the crew to get out. Suddenly, King found himself outside the Dakota as it broke up. An instant later his parachute opened with a crack that caused him to part company with his shoes. He came to earth in no-man's land and succeeded in joining up with the 10th Parachute Battalion, which was part of Brigadier John Hackett's 4th Parachute Brigade and which was trying to hold Wolfheze railway station. King obtained a Sten gun and fought alongside the paratroops until the next morning, when the survivors were forced to surrender.

* * * *

A fighter pilot attacks an enemy aircraft that has been shadowing a convoy of merchant ships. Whether he is successful or not, he must then either ditch his fighter or bale out into the freezing waters of the North Atlantic, knowing that if he is not picked up quickly, he will die.

That was the unenviable game of chance that faced one gallant band of British airmen in the Second World War. Drawn from both the Royal Air Force and the Fleet Air Arm, they belonged to the Merchant Ship Fighter Unit (MSFU), which was hastily organised in 1941 to combat shore-based, long-range German aircraft like the Focke-Wulf Fw 200 Kondor, which were inflicting serious losses on Britain's vital Atlantic convoys. A number of merchant ships were equipped with catapults and designated Catapult Aircraft Merchantmen (CAMs). Each carried a Hawker Hurricane or Fairey Fulmar fighter, mounted on the catapult. The latter was rocket-powered and the acceleration subjected aircraft and pilot to three and a half g, during which the pilot had to keep sufficient wits about him to control the fighter as it reached flying speed dangerously close to the stall. The technique was to use one-third starboard rudder to counteract the aircraft's tendency to swing to port, with one-third flap and the elevator and trimming tabs neutral. A further essential precaution was to jam the right elbow hard into the hip to avoid jerking the stick, because too much backward pressure would cause the Hurricane to stall into the sea.

By the end of the first week in July 1941 twenty-five Sea Hurricanes had been delivered to the Merchant Ship Fighter Unit and sixteen CAM ships had sailed. Four catapult-equipped naval auxiliary vessels were also in service, and it was from one of these, the *Maplin*, on 18 July 1941, that a Sea Hurricane flown by Lieutenant R.W. H. Everett RNVR intercepted a Focke-Wulf Kondor which had just bombed and set fire to a ship. As he closed in for the kill, some gunners on another ship blew away part of the Kondor's starboard wing and the four-engined aircraft crashed into the sea. Luckily, Everett had enough fuel to reach Northern Ireland, where he landed safely.

On 31 July, with Everett once again one of the three naval pilots on board, *Maplin* sailed to meet a convoy homeward bound from Sierra Leone, and on 2 August Everett happened to be the duty pilot when a Kondor was sighted away to the south. This time there was no mistake. Overhauling the Kondor with painful slowness, for the Hurricane was only a few miles an hour faster than the enemy aircraft, Everett skilfully manoeuvred through heavy defensive gunfire and shot the Focke-Wulf down. He subsequently ditched his Hurricane, rather than bale out, and had a hard time getting clear of the cockpit under water before he broke surface to be picked up by an escorting destroyer. His exploit brought him a well-earned Distinguished Service Order.

The first RAF Sea Hurricane pilot to engage a Kondor was Pilot Officer G.W. Varley, who was launched from the CAM ship SS *Empire Foam* on 1 November 1941 to intercept an Fw 200 that was shadowing Convoy HX 156, homeward bound from Halifax. The Kondor escaped in cloud and Varley baled out to be picked up frozen but unharmed and dumped into a hot bath, clothing and all, aboard the destroyer HMS *Broke*.

Rocket-assisted take-off: a Sea Hurricane blasts off the catapult of a CAM ship during trials. (IWM)

End of a convoy shadower: a Blohm und Voss Bv 138 takes its final plunge towards the Atlantic after being attacked by a British fighter. (Author's collection)

In the spring of 1942, CAM ships were assigned to Russian convoys for the first time. On 25 May, Flying Officer John Kendal was launched from the SS *Empire Morn* – part of the westbound Convoy PQ.12 – to intercept a Blohm und Voss Bv 138 flying boat; this he failed to do, but he chased and shot down a Junkers Ju 88 soon afterwards. Sadly, Kendal did not live to celebrate his victory. He baled out but his parachute failed to deploy properly, and he was dead when a rescue craft reached him.

On that same day another Hurricane pilot, Flying Officer A.J. 'Al' Hay, a South African, was heading east towards Murmansk on the SS *Empire Lawrence*, which was part of Convoy PQ.16. The two convoys had, in fact, passed within sight of one another midway between Jan Mayen and Bear islands. In the early evening, PQ 16 was attacked by a large number of Ju 88 and Heinkel He 111 torpedo-bombers, and Hay was launched to do what he could. He attacked a formation of four Heinkels, destroying one and damaging another, but his aircraft was hit in the engagement and he was wounded in the thigh by shell splinters. Nevertheless, he abandoned his Hurricane successfully and was picked up by a destroyer after six minutes in the water. Forty-eight hours later, the *Empire Lawrence* was torpedoed and sunk in another heavy air attack; this time, there was no Hurricane to defend the convoy.

On 14 June, a Kondor was intercepted by Pilot Officer A.V. Sanders, launched from the SS *Empire Moon* in the course of a homeward run from Gibraltar. The enemy aircraft was damaged, but got away. Flying Officer A.H. Burr had better luck on 16 September, when Convoy PQ 18, bound for Russia, was attacked by torpedo-carrying He 111s. Burr used up all his ammunition in an attack on an He 111 and, although he failed to see it go down, had the satisfaction of seeing both its engines stream white smoke before he was forced to break off. He landed safely at Keg Ostrov, near Archangel'sk.

On 25 October, 1942, a Focke-Wulf Fw 200 was destroyed by Flying Officer Norman Taylor, whose Hurricane was launched from the SS *Empire Heath* as she steamed with a convoy out of Gibraltar. The action took place about 300 miles north-west of the Portuguese coast. Taylor had a difficult interception, because the Kondor was flying low over the sea and the German pilot, who clearly knew his business, kept turning so that the reflection of sunlight from the water always dazzled his opponent. However, Taylor persisted, attacking from astern through heavy defensive fire, and at last the big aircraft went down into the sea. Taylor, who – unknown to his colleagues – was a non-swimmer, had an anxious time when he became entangled in his parachute under water following a successful bale-out, but he managed to extricate himself and was picked up. He was awarded a Distinguished Flying Cross.

CAM ship operations continued into the summer of 1943, and they ended in a blaze of glory at the very moment when the MSFU was being disbanded. On 23 July, the last two CAM ships in service, the *Empire Tide* and the *Empire Darwin*, both sailed with Convoy SL 133, homeward bound from Gibraltar on the last leg of a voyage from Sierra Leone. In the evening of 28 July, Pilot Officer J.A. Stewart was catapulted from the *Empire Darwin* and made a successful attack on a Focke-Wulf Fw 200 before his guns jammed, after which he climbed to make several dummy attacks on a second Kondor, frustrating its bombing run over the convoy. It was later confirmed that the first Kondor had crashed in the sea. Meanwhile, Pilot Officer P.J.R. Flynn had also been launched from the second CAM ship, the *Empire Tide*, and made a determined attack on yet another Kondor through heavy return fire, driving the enemy aircraft away with one of its engines smoking. Flynn was credited with one damaged; both he and Stewart were picked up safely.

This action demonstrated the value of the CAM ship concept as never before, but by this time the men of the MSFU were already dispersing to other units. In just over two years of operations, the CAM ships had undertaken 175 voyages. The total number of Hurricanes involved, exactly matching the vessels available, had been thirty-five. There had been eight operational launchings, resulting in the destruction of six enemy aircraft and the driving off of several others. Only one Hurricane pilot, John Kendal, had lost his life.

In fact, the value of the CAM ship concept had been considerable. Quite apart from the presence of the Hurricanes acting as a deterrent to attacking aircraft, the very sight of them, perched on their catapults, had provided a great morale booster for the merchant seamen. One sailor, Leading Seaman Gunlayer H.P. Hough of Liverpool, who saw John Kendal's fatal descent into the sea, speaks for them all.

He was my wartime hero. I only wish I could have met his family, to tell them what a debt we owed to those pilots...

CHAPTER FIVE

THE 'BANG SEAT'

O n the night of 5/6 January, 1945, Squadron Leader Lewis Brandon and Flight Lieutenant James Benson, flying an intruder operation in a de Havilland Mosquito over northern Germany, had been following a radar contact which, disappointingly, turned out to be a Lancaster bomber when Brandon suddenly picked up another trace on his radar screen. Whatever the strange aircraft was, it proved very hard to catch, climbing fast towards Hannover. Benson finally caught it at a range of half a mile over the burning city and identified it as a Heinkel 219, easily recognisable because of its twin fins and array of radar aerials. Benson crept up behind the enemy aircraft and opened fire at 200 yards, hitting the Heinkel's engines. Large pieces broke off and it went down in a steep dive, with the Mosquito following. At 6000 feet the enemy night fighter entered a steep climb up to 12,000 feet, where it heeled over and dived almost vertically into the ground.

Benson and Brandon were puzzled by the enemy aircraft's erratic behaviour after the attack, as they had not seen the crew bale out. Later, they learned that the He 219 was equipped with ejection seats – the first aircraft in the world to employ them operationally. It may well have been the case that on this occasion, the German crew had used them, and that two of the large pieces the Mosquito crew had seen break away had, in fact, been the seats punching out of the Heinkel.

The *Luftwaffe*'s Aviation Medicine Section, in fact, had been experimenting with ejection escape systems before the outbreak of World War Two. Many tests were carried out to determine what forces of gravity and acceleration the human body was capable of withstanding, such tests being prompted by the need to ensure adequate escape for the crew of dive-bombers like the Junkers Ju 87 *Stuka*, which experienced sustained high G loading as it pulled out of its dive.

The responsibility for designing and perfecting such early escape systems was assigned to the Heinkel aircraft company, which in 1936 had begun design work on a rocket-powered aircraft, the He 176. In this aircraft, the entire glazed nose section, in which the pilot sat on a reclined couch, could be jettisoned in an emergency by means of compressed air. A main parachute would then deploy and decelerate the nose section to the point where it was safe for the pilot to bale out conventionally. To test the system, a cockpit mock-up with a dummy pilot inside was dropped from a Heinkel He 111 at altitudes of up to 22,000 feet. The system was never fully developed, mainly because of problems with the main parachute deployment and because it was found that the minimum safe height for cockpit separation was over 19,000

The Heinkel He 280, seen here on an early test flight with engine cowlings removed, was fitted with one of the company's ejection seats. (Author's collection)

feet. However, it was determined that a pilot would stand a good chance of survival if he remained strapped in the nose section as it descended under its parachute.

The He 176, which flew under rocket power for the first time on 30 June 1939, was followed by the He 178, which first flew on 27 August 1939 and which was the first aircraft in the world powered solely by a turbojet engine. This did not have an ejection seat, but Heinkel's next turbojet-powered design, the twin-engined He 280, did.

Experiments so far had shown that the human body was capable of withstanding about +20G for a duration of 0.1 second. The German preference at this time was for a compressed-gas system of ejecting the aircrew seat, although explosive-cartridge propelled seats were also under development. The explosive seat developed by Heinkel consisted of a bucket seat assembly mounted on four rollers which moved in two parallel runners 42 inches in length. The seat was fired by means of a catapult tube; this was in two components, the lower one attached to the airframe and the upper one to the top of the seat. On pulling a handle, the pilot detonated an explosive charge, which propelled the seat out of the cockpit after the canopy had been jettisoned manually. Ejection velocity was thirty-five feet per second, the pilot experiencing an acceleration of 12G. The compressed air escape system had an ejection velocity of 57 feet per second and an acceleration of 27G, which meant that any pilot using it was likely to sustain serious spinal injuries. It was also prohibitively heavy and presented considerable field maintenance problems.

It was a compressed- air-type seat that was fitted to the Heinkel He 280, and it was used in earnest during a test flight of the He 280V1 on 13 January 1943. The He 280V1 had been sent to the experimental flight test centre at Rechlin to test the Argus As 014 pulse jet, intended for the Fieseler Fi 103 (V-1) flying bomb. It was flown on this occasion by an Argus test pilot, a man named Schenck. With four As 014s mounted under its wings, the He 280 was incapable of taking off under its own power, and two Bf 110 twin-engined fighters acted as tugs. The one and only flight ended in disaster. Snow clouds which rose from the runway completely obscured the He 280 pilot's visibility, and he soon found that he was unable to release the tow lines. Neither was he ale to communicate with the pilots of the tug aircraft, who were unaware of his predicament. Finally, at 9000 feet the pilot was no longer able to control his overladen aircraft and ejected, and the He 280V1, at last released by its tugs, crashed into a nearby forest. Although Schenck's was the first known use of an ejection seat for emergency egress, the Heinkel compressed air seat used by Schenck had purportedly been tested earlier in an experimental ejection from a trials aircraft by a Heinkel employee named Busch.

Heinkel remained responsible for ejection seat development in Germany throughout the war, and by late 1942 all German experimental aircraft were equipped with some form of ejection seat while being flight tested. The first operational aircraft to be fitted with ejection seats was the Heinkel He 219 night fighter, and the device was subsequently to save the lives of several aircrew.

The Heinkel He 219

In the first half of 1943, General Kammhuber, commanding Germany's night-fighter defences, pressed strongly for the production of new twin-engined types designed specifically for night fighting. At the forefront of these was the Heinkel He 219 Uhu (Owl), the prototype of which had flown in November 1942 after months of delay caused by a lack of interest on the part of the German Air Ministry. By April 1943 300 examples had been ordered; Kammhuber wanted 2000, but in the event only 294 were built before the end of the war. Formidably armed with six 20mm cannon and equipped with the latest AI radar, the He 219 would certainly have torn great gaps in the ranks of the RAF's night bombers had it been available in quantity. It also had a performance comparable to that of the Mosquito, which other German night fighters did not, and could therefore have fought the RAF's night intruders on equal terms. Admittedly, the He 219 suffered from a series of technical troubles in its early development career, but what it might have achieved in action was ably demonstrated on the night of 11/12 June 1943 by Major Werner Streib of I/NJG 1. Flying a pre-production He 219 on operational trials from Venlo, he infiltrated an RAF bomber stream heading for Berlin and shot down five Lancasters in half an hour. The only sour note for Streib sounded when the flaps of the He 219 failed to function and the aircraft overran the runway on landing, breaking into three pieces. Streib and his observer escaped without injury.

The He 219 was conceived as a private venture in the summer of 1940, the intention being to produce a multi-role combat aircraft. The

---

problems experienced by Ernst Heinkel AG in bringing the design to operational fruition were compounded when, in March 1942, over three-quarters of the drawings were destroyed in a night attack by the RAF on the Heinkel works at Rostock. As well as the night fighter variant, Heinkel intended to produce the He 219A-1 reconnaissance bomber, the He 219A-3 high-speed bomber, and the He 219A-4 high altitude reconnaissance aircraft with long-span wooden wings, but these projects were abandoned and production concentrated on the He 219A-2 night fighter. In May 1944, however, General Field Marshal Milch, in charge of aircraft production, persuaded the German Air Ministry to abandon the He 219 in favour of two new night fighters, the Junkers Ju 388J, which in the event never went into operational service, and the Focke-Wulf Ta 154, an all-wooden design which was prone to structural failure. As a consequence of this disastrous decision, the He 219, which was readily available and had already proven itself to be a lethal weapon, saw service only in limited numbers.

The He 219 was universally popular with both air and ground crews, and introduced several new features. Apart from being the first combat aircraft to be fitted with ejection seats, it was the first operational German aircraft to feature a tricycle undercarriage, and the fact that the armament was concentrated behind the pilot, in the wing roots and in a ventral tray, prevented him from being temporarily blinded when the weapons were fired. Various armament installations were tested in the He 219 sub-variants; the he 219A-7/R1, for example, had no fewer than eight cannon, two MK 108s in the wing roots, two MK 103s and two MG 151/20s in the ventral tray and two MK 108s in a Shräge Musik installation aft of the cockpit, firing obliquely upwards.

Other German aircraft to be fitted with ejection seats were the Dornier Do 335, the Heinkel He 162, the Arado Ar 234B, the Messerschmitt Me 163 and the Messerschmitt Me 262. In the case of the Me 163, the seat was a spring-loaded device. Rather surprisingly, not all Messerschmitt Me 262 jet fighters were fitted with ejection seats, and the principal reason for fitting ejection seats in the Heinkel He 162 *Volksjäger* was that the pilot's cockpit was situated directly in front of the turbojet engine, which was mounted on top of the fuselage.

It was a similar story with the Dornier 335, which had its engines mounted in tandem and, initially, a rather complex procedure for abandoning the aircraft in an emergency. The rear propeller and upper tail fin were jettisoned, followed by the cockpit canopy, and the pilot then left the aircraft by conventional means. With the Do 335, however, there was an additional danger. The pilot had to reach up with both hands to jettison the canopy, which was then ripped off by the slipstream. Unfortunately, if the aircraft was travelling at speed, so were the pilot's arms.

In Sweden, Saab also encountered problems in devising a safe escape system

The Arado Ar 234B jet bomber was one of the types fitted with an ejection seat. (Author's collection)

for their J-21 piston-engined fighter, which had twin tail booms and a 'pusher' engine. After various systems had been considered and rejected, Saab carried out ground trials with a compressed air-type seat; this produced an acceleration of around 20G, but the human guinea pig suffered no ill effects and the seat underwent airborne trials in 1942, being fired from a Junkers Ju 86 with a dummy pilot strapped into it. The seat and dummy cleared the aircraft's tail unit by fifteen feet.

Like the Germans before them, Saab found that the compressed air system was too heavy and complicated, so the company entered into collaboration with Bofors to produce an alternative, and in 1943 an explosive-type seat was subjected to successful ground trials. Known as the Saab Mk I, this seat produced an acceleration of 15G. The ejection sequence was initiated by a handle on the right side of the instrument panel, which on being pulled jettisoned the canopy and armed the seat. Radio and oxygen lines were severed by a guillotine. After ejection the seat straps were disconnected

It was only towards the end of its operational life that the Me 262 jet fighter was fitted with an ejection seat. (Author's collection)

The Saab J 21A was the first Swedish fighter to be fitted with an ejection seat. (Saab)

automatically, but the parachute had to be opened manually. The seat was air-tested from a Saab B-17 on 27 February 1944, being ejected at 4000 feet at a speed of 250mph.

The seat was installed in the first production Saab J-21A fighter, which flew on 1 June 1945. By this time the seat had been modified by moving the ejection handle to above the left shoulder and shoulder straps had been introduced, only a seat belt having been used previously. The first emergency ejection in Sweden occurred on 29 July 1946, when a Saab J 21A collided with an FFVS J 22 fighter. The first ejection from the jet-powered version of the J 21A, the Saab J 21R, was on 28 March 1948. In all there were twenty-five ejections from both variants of the Saab 21, of which twenty-three were successful, from a total of 302 aircraft in service from 1945 to 1956.

Ejection seats were also fitted to the Saab B-18 bomber, after the type had been in service for some time, because of its bad safety record. Of 244 aircraft built, forty-four were destroyed in accidents between 1944 and 1959, and only four of these accidents ended with crew members escaping from the aircraft, despite the pilots having the benefit of ejection seats from as early as 1949. It may be (as was later the case with RAF jet bombers) that pilots chose to stay with the aircraft rather than save themselves while other crew members perished.

In the United States, at the end of the Second World War, the Heinkel ejection-seat system was examined as a possible means of providing safe exit from the USAAF's new Lockheed P-80 Shooting Star jet fighter, but its velocity was found to be insufficient. The basic Heinkel design was modified by the USAAF's Engineering Division at Wright Field (later Wright-Patterson Air Force Base) and this resulted in a prototype American seat, which was successfully fired, with a live volunteer (Sergeant Lawrence Lambert) strapped in, from a modified Northrop P-61 Black Widow on 17 August 1946.

After further development of the concept the seat was installed in the P-80, and in 1949 the Republic F-84 Thunderjet became the first American production aircraft to have ejection seats fitted from the outset. The early American seats, following the German pattern, used an armrest-actuating trigger, which had to be raised and then squeezed. Although a conventional seat-type parachute was at first used in the original American seat (used in the P-80), a back-type parachute was later incorporated. Seat separation had to be achieved manually, the pilot freeing himself from the ejected seat first, then manually deploying his personal back-type chute after physically pushing himself away from the seat. Only later did refinements come to be incorporated into the system, which included leg restraint provisions, correct separation sequencing, and fully automatic seat-separations – all or most of these having been addressed, or at least recognised as desirable, early on by the Martin-Baker Company in Britain.

The Martin-Baker Aircraft Company Ltd was founded as an aircraft manufacturer in 1934 by James (later Sir James) Martin and Captain Valentine Baker and went on to produce four combat aircraft prototypes, none of which was selected for RAF service. On 12 September 1942 Captain Baker was killed testing one of them, the MB.3.

In 1944, James Martin was invited by the then Ministry of Aircraft Production to investigate the feasibility of providing fighter aircraft with a means of assisted escape for the pilot, the need for such a system having been accentuated by the death, on 4 January 1944, of Squadron Leader W.D.B.S. Davie AFC, who lost his life while testing the Gloster F.9/40, the prototype Meteor jet fighter. During a high-speed run at 20,000 feet, the port Metropolitan Vickers engine disintegrated over Farnborough. The pilot lost his left arm while attempting to remove the cockpit canopy, and on making his exit over the side collided with the tailplane. His body fell through the roof of the parachute packing section, just missing the man who had packed his parachute the day before.

The earliest prototype Martin-Baker seats were configured with the parachute pack in the seat pan and the sea survival pack and inflatable raft fitted behind the back. This was also the configuration for the earliest production model, the Martin-Baker Mk.1 seat. It was found, however, that this configuration increased the risk of spinal injury on ejection, and in subsequent marks, the parachute was moved to a position behind the back, with the sea survival kit stowed in the seat-pan.

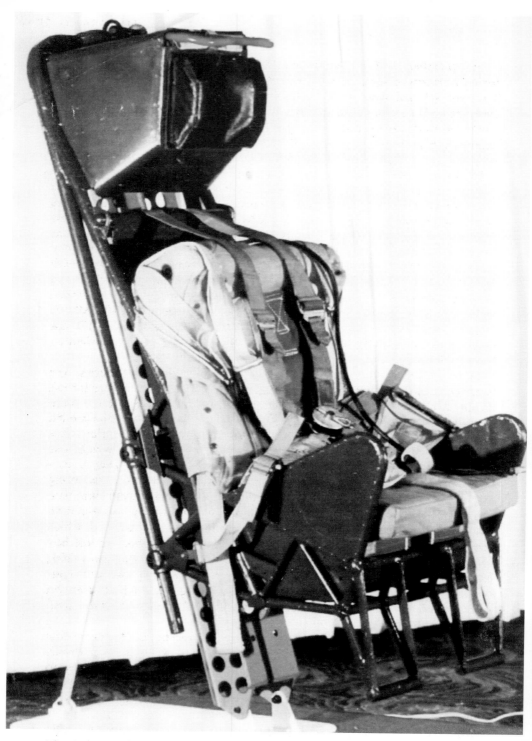

The Martin-Baker Mk 1 ejection seat was initially configured with a back-type parachute pack. (Martin-Baker)

In September 1945, the Ministry of Aircraft production placed a contract for two prototype seats, which would be air-tested in a high-speed aircraft. The type selected was the Meteor Mk 3, and after a number of dummy ejections and corresponding modifications of such components as the drogue chute and its deployment device (a gun was incorporated in place of a spring deployment mechanism), the first British live ejection test was made by test subject Bernard Lynch on 24 July 1946.

In June of 1947 the decision was made in England to fit the new Martin-Baker ejection seat (Mark 1) to all British tactical military aircraft. A number of versions of the original Mk.1 seat were produced for a variety of jet fighters and bombers. Various small changes in the Mark 1 application for each aircraft type reflected the unique requirements or constraints of that particular aircraft. The Meteor fighter was initially fitted with the M-B Mk.1, and later with the Mk.1E seat. The Royal Navy's Vickers-Supermarine Attacker was fitted with the Mk.1A (it was later upgraded to the M-B Mk.2A model). The Westland Wyvern naval strike fighter was fitted with the Mk.1B model (later upgraded to Mk.2B). The English Electric Canberra jet bomber received the M-B Mk.1C seat, and the Hawker Seahawk aircraft was fitted with the M-B Mk.1D seat (later upgraded to M-B Mk.2D seat). The M-B Mk.1F seat went to the new de Havilland Venom fighter (later upgraded to the M-B Mk.2F seat).

Prior to full-scale production of the Martin-Baker Mk.1 series, the Saunders-Roe Aviation Company placed an order for an ejection seat for use on its Saro A-1 jet flying boat fighter. This seat lacked some of the more sophisticated features and detailing of the standard Mk.1 production model, and was officially designated the Pre-Mark 1 Seat. Altogether the Mk.1 production seat weighed some 172 pounds (143 pounds of which was ejectable). Its innovations included a two-cartridge ejection gun; a gas-pressure release mechanism unlocking the ejection piston from the firing cylinder immediately upon firing of the first cartridge; an adjustable seat pan; spring-loaded footrests to facilitate foot placement for ejection; a face-curtain seat actuation system, which assured proper ejection posture and which protected the pilot's face from blast injury; an explosive drogue gun method of deploying the seat's stabilising drogue chute; retractable seat-pan raising handle; the Martin-Baker back-type sea survival/dinghy pack, and seat-cushion type personal parachute; and integral thigh restraining seat-pan extrusions. By 1950, the Mark 1 series seat was standard on all first line RAF and RN fighters.

The early Martin-Baker seat was also selected for use by the US Navy's first generation of jet fighters, the Navy having decided in 1946 that the British company's research and development programme was so far advanced as to make parallel work in the United States a waste of resources. The US Navy therefore arranged to produce a slightly modified seat for naval use, together with technical support facilities.

The first man in Britain to save his life by using an ejection seat was Flight Lieutenant J.O. Lancaster, a test pilot with Armstrong Whitworth Aircraft.

Lancaster had a distinguished Service career behind him, having been awarded the DFC while serving with RAF Bomber Command. At this time, his principal task was to test a revolutionary new aircraft, the Armstrong Whitworth AW.52 jet-powered flying wing.

During the Second World War, Armstrong Whitworth had proposed a jet-powered four-engined 120-foot span laminar-flow flying-wing bomber. The design was to be evaluated through the use of a one-third scale glider. The end of the war brought an end to the project but not before work had started on the AW.52G glider, which first flew on 2 March 1945. Armstrong Whitworth, after cancellation of the bomber project, maintained its interest in a large flying wing and was eventually given a contract to produce two jet-powered prototypes. To give some point to the project beyond research the type was designed to carry 4,000 pounds of mail. The first Nene-powered aircraft flew on 13 November 1947 and eventually achieved speeds of around 500mph.

On 30 May, 1949, 'Jo' Lancaster took off from the Armstrong Whitworth aerodrome at Bitteswell, near Rugby, on his third flight in the AW.52. Having completed his sortie task, Lancaster began the let-down for a landing at Bitteswell, and was passing through 15,000 feet when he encountered trouble. Suddenly, Lancaster felt himself lifted out of his seat against the Sutton harness. Just as abruptly he was forced back into his seat again. The flying wing had, unaccountably, started a most violent fore and aft pitching movement. Rapidly the oscillations built up until they reached a terrifying level. Lancaster found his hands and feet being jerked from the controls. His vision was becoming blurred.

So violently was Lancaster shaken up that he could not later remember what action he took in an attempt to dampen the pitching or to reduce speed. His last clear recollection was of the airspeed indicator showing 320 knots and the altimeter reading 5000 feet. In a few seconds Lancaster would be rendered unconscious by the shaking; he knew that he had to get out.

At that time the AW.52 was one of the few aircraft to be fitted with one of Martin-Baker's new ejection seats. Lancaster, without the possibility that the seat might not work even crossing his mind, initiated the ejection procedure. First he had to pull the handle to jettison the cockpit canopy. This also severed the control rods and allowed the control wheel to move forward from its position in the pilot's lap so that he could eject safely. Then he was to pull down the blind which covered his face and fired the ejection cartridge. Then, if all went to plan, he would be shot safely from the aircraft.

But there was also a third handle. This jettisoned the canopy, but did not sever the control rods. Lancaster, near unconsciousness, pulled the wrong handle, with the result that the control wheel was not free when he pulled the blind to eject himself. He was saved from terrible injury to his legs only by a miracle. As he shot from the cockpit, the pitching of the aircraft moved the control column forward sufficiently to give his lower body free passage.

He was at last free of the disintegrating aircraft, but he still had to detach himself from his seat. This was a simple enough operation, but as he pulled the ripcord of his parachute, the discarded seat came hurtling past him, far too close for comfort. A twenty-knot wind and a pendulum swing which

The Armstrong Whitworth AW.52 flying wing, from which test pilot J.O. Lancaster successfully ejected in May 1949. (Jacques Trempe collection).

developed when he attempted to steer himself away from a canal gave him a heavy landing which kept him away from flying for three months. Lancaster came down at Long Itchington, 6 miles east of Leamington. After he abandoned the aircraft it stabilised itself and made a slow descent into a field, where it struck the only large tree in the vicinity with the leading edge of the starboard wing, outboard of the engine intake. It then slid along the ground for half a mile, disintegrating as it went.

Lancaster had been extremely lucky to escape with his life. As a result of this accident it was quickly appreciated that the escape system was too complicated, and steps were taken to improve and simplify it. The first and possibly most obvious requirement was for the automatic release of the occupant, who would be unable to release himself manually if he were injured or unconscious. The second was the difficulty in judging the correct height for parachute deployment. These requirements were met in the Martin-Baker Mk 2 seat by fitting a clockwork timer that was activated on ejection. At the end of 5 seconds, the drogue chute was disconnected from the seat by the use of a scissor shackle. As it pulled away, it was connected to an apron-like static line which tipped the seat occupant forward and it caused the main parachute to be deployed. The operation of the timer was inhibited by an aneroid capsule which blocked the running of the clockwork release. On reaching a predetermined height (usually 10,000 feet above sea level) the clockwork mechanism was allowed to run freely, permitting the scissor shackle to operate and in turn allow the drogue to separate from the seat, pulling out the pilot's main parachute. Early Mark 1 seats were retrofitted to Mk 2 standard.

Although the Mk 2 seat was a great improvement, faster aircraft were being introduced where a higher ejection trajectory would be needed to clear the tail. This need was underlined in tragic fashion on 12 January 1952, when a Royal Air Force officer, Squadron Leader Brian Foster, was flying as co-pilot in the prototype Vickers Valiant, the first of the RAF's V-bombers, carrying out engine shutdown and relight trials over the Hampshire coast. Fire broke out

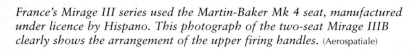

France's Mirage III series used the Martin-Baker Mk 4 seat, manufactured under licence by Hispano. This photograph of the two-seat Mirage IIIB clearly shows the arrangement of the upper firing handles. (Aerospatiale)

The Martin-Baker Mk 5 seat in action. In this remarkable photograph, showing a US Navy pilot ejecting from an F-8 Crusader, the time release mechanism (TRM) has released the drogue shackle and it has begun to pull the main parachute out of its pack. The TRM has also released the leg restraint attachments and the survival kit latches, permitting the pilot to fall forward away from the seat. The pilot's personal parachute has also been freed from the seat. (US Navy)

in an engine bay as the result of a wet start, and as no fire detection equipment had been installed in the bay, by the time the blaze was detected the damage was so advanced that the wing was on the point of collapse. The pilot therefore gave the order to abandon the aircraft and the three rear crew members went out first, followed by the two pilots. All the crew survived with the exception of Sqn Ldr Foster, who was killed when his seat struck the fin while the aircraft was in a descending turn. To avoid accidents of this kind Martin-Baker developed the Mk 3 seat, which produced an ejection velocity of 80 feet per second instead of 60 fps by using a telescopic ejection gun with a stroke of 72 inches.

Further developments by Martin-Baker produced the Mk 4 lightweight seat, considered as the first of the second-generation seats. It was fitted to some 35 different types of aircraft, the the first emergency ejection being from a Fiat G 91 in March 1957.

The Mk 5 seat was basically a Mk 4 for the United States Navy, strengthened to withstand deceleration loads of 40g instead of the 25g British specification. The seats were also fitted with canopy breaker lugs on top of the drogue box to facilitate ejecting through the canopy. Due to the success of the Mk. 5 seats it was decided to standardise the fitting of Martin-Baker seats in all US Navy aircraft, a trend which continues to this day.

A big step forward came with the development of the Mks 6 and 7. The addition of a rocket assembly to the basic designs converted the Mk 4 to Mk 6 and the Mk 5 to Mk 7 standard. The Mk 7 seat was further modified as other improvements were added such as power retraction, which pulled aircrew into a suitable posture for ejection. Many thousands were made and were fitted to aircraft such as the F-4 Phantom, F-14 Tomcat, and F-8U Crusader. The addition of the rocket pack gave the seat a true zero-zero capability, fired the ejectee to a height of about 350 feet, sufficient for the drogues to pull out and deploy the personal parachute.

CHAPTER SIX

COMBAT OVER KOREA

O f all the aircrews who flew and fought in Korea from 1950 to 1953, those who ran some of the greatest risks were the crews of the light aircraft and helicopters of the air rescue squadrons, flying deep behind enemy lines to snatch shot-down pilots to safety.

On the outbreak of war in Korea there were two search and rescue units at the disposal of Far East Air Force (FEAF); these were the 2nd and 3rd Air Rescue Squadrons, the former serving the Thirteenth and Twentieth Air Forces and the latter under the operational control of the Fifth Air Force. Naturally enough, it was the Japan-based 3rd Squadron that was to bear the brunt of air rescue operations in Korea. The Squadron's equipment at the outbreak of hostilities consisted of SB-17s and a number of Sikorsky H-5 (S-51) helicopters, but on 28 July 1950 three Grumman SA-16 Albatross amphibians were added to the inventory. Along with the SB-17s, these patrolled the Tsushima Straits between Korea and Japan, ready to go to the assistance of any ditched pilot. On 7 July, 1950, the 3rd Squadron sent two L-5 liaison

The Sikorsky H5 (S-51) helicopter saved the lives of many shot-down UN aircrew during the Korean War.
(Sikorsky)

aircraft to carry out 'snatches' from inside enemy territory. Their rescue attempts, however, were hampered by the fact that they were quite unsuited to operating from the sodden paddy fields of the battle area. The situation changed for the better on 22 July, with the arrival at Taegu airstrip of the first detachment of H-5s. Within a few days the helicopters were being used to evacuate badly wounded soldiers of the Eighth Army from the mountainous or rice paddy terrain of the front line to hospitals in Miryang and Pusan. These operations were so successful that Major General General Earle E. Partridge, commanding the US Fifth Air Force, directed the 3rd Squadron to position six of its nine H-5s in Korea. At the same time, General George E. Stratemeyer, Commander-in-Chief of the Far East Air Forces, asked the USAF to allocate 25 more H-5s to form a special duties and evacuation unit, and within a fortnight fourteen helicopters were on their way to Korea.

By this time Marine Corps Observation Squadron VMO-6 was also operational at the front, and its HO-3 helicopters began operations on 3 August 1950 in support of the 1st Marine Division in the Changwon area, delivering rations and water to troops in mountain positions and evacuating heat-stroke cases. By the end of August 1950 the 3rd Air Rescue Squadron's helicopters had flown eighty-three badly wounded soldiers from the battle area. All of them would almost certainly have died had they been forced to make the journey to a field hospital by ambulance. The Squadron's operations were now co-ordinated by a Rescue Liaison Office, which had been set up in the United Nations Command Joint Operations Centre on 27 August, and it was while under the control of the Liaison Office that one of the unit's H-5s made history. It happened on the morning of 4 September, 1950, when two flights of Lockheed F-80 Shooting Stars of the 35th Fighter-Bomber Squadron crossed the 38th Parallel, the demarcation line separating North and South Korea, to attack targets at Hanggandong. During the attack, one of the F-80s was shot down; the pilot, Captain Robert E. Wayne, baled out and landed safely. While two of the F-80s circled the area on the lookout for North Korean troops, a third climbed and made radio contact with base. Half an hour later, while a flight of F-80s flew combat air patrol overhead to ward off any enemy fighters, Captain Wayne was on his way out of enemy territory in an H-5. It was flown by Lieutenant Paul W. Van Boven, who had just become the first ever helicopter pilot to lift a shot-down airman to safety from behind enemy lines.

The H-5 unit, now designated Detachment F and commanded by Captain Oscar N. Tibbetts, moved forward in support of UN forces counter-attacking northwards from the Pusan Perimeter towards the end of September 1950, arriving at Seoul during the first week of October. It was from this base that, on 10 October, the longest helicopter rescue mission so far was flown when an H-5 piloted by Lieutenant David C. McDaniels made a 125-mile flight to Changjon to pick up the wounded pilot of a Sea Fury, shot down during a sortie from the British aircraft carrier HMS *Theseus*. The British pilot was Lieutenant S. Leonard of No 807 Squadron, who was brought down while

The Lockheed F-80 Shooting Star, seen here taking off with rocket assistance, was the real workhorse of the war in Korea. (International News)

The F-80 could sustain a great deal of battle damage and still return to base, as this photograph indicates. (Author's collection) making a rocket attack on enemy troops 90 miles behind the lines. The fuselage of his aircraft buckled at the cockpit, trapping him with both legs and one arm broken. He was also knocked unconscious. His flight, and a relief flight, strafed enemy soldiers and prevented them from getting near the crashed Sea Fury. Leonard came to, fired his revolver – with his broken arm – at the nearest enemy, then passed out again. The H-5 arrived after about an hour, carrying a doctor as well as the pilot, and the two men hacked Leonard free while keeping the enemy at bay with bursts from their automatic weapons. The Fleet Air Arm officer received a blood transfusion in the helicopter on the homeward flight, and subsequently made a full recovery.

Several more long-range rescue flights were made during November 1950 by H-5s operating from advanced bases at Kunu-ri and Sinanju. Then came the Chinese invasion, compelling Detachment F to pull its forward elements back to Seoul, and when Seoul was evacuated in its turn the helicopters moved to Airstrip K-37, south of Taegu. By the end of 1950 the H-5s had transported 618 medical cases, compared with 56 flown out by the fixed-wing L-5s.

It was a Stinson L-5 that came to the rescue of Lieutenant Tracy B. Mathewson, a USAF pilot who, in the late afternoon of 11 December 1950, was flying in a formation of four F-80 Shooting Star jets on an offensive mission over North Korea. Racing low over the snow-covered terrain, the pilots spotted a pair of North Korean Yakovlev Yak-9 fighters climbing away from Pyongyang airport. They seemed an easy target and Mathewson pushed open the throttle, at the same time flicking off the safety catch of his machine guns. Perhaps, he thought, this was the moment he had been waiting for: the chance to score his first 'kill' over Korea.

But Mathewson's world suddenly turned upside down as a shattering explosion tore his F-80 apart. The jet skidded violently across the sky and the pilot was hurled brutally against the side of the cockpit as the fighter flicked over on its back. He snatched a glance rearwards. Where the tail should have been there was nothing; the F-80 had been torn in half by an anti-aircraft burst. He had to eject, and fast. He groped for the hood jettison release and pulled it. The perspex canopy flew off with a bang and a blast of air roared into the cockpit, blinding him. The aircraft rolled as another explosion shook it. A dark shadow flashed past the cockpit. It was the wing, torn completely from the fuselage. Frantically, Mathewson groped for the ejection seat handle. The next instant, without knowing how it had happened, he found himself spreadeagled in mid-air, detached from his seat, falling amid a cloud of debris. Desperately, he tore at his parachute's D-ring. A strip of silk the size of a pocket handkerchief fluttered from his parachute pack. He had no time to feel fear; there was a hazy impression of the earth whirling up to meet him, a violent shock, and then oblivion.

A few hundred feet above, the other three American jets, the enemy fighters forgotten, swept over the spot where Mathewson had hit the ground and circled over the wreck of his F-80. The pilots could see Mathewson's body, his Mae West lifejacket a bright patch of yellow against the churned-up snow and mud. Then, incredibly, they saw the downed pilot sit up and wave to them.

Mathewson released his unopened parachute, scrambled to his feet and felt his body cautiously to see if anything was broken. Apart from a dull ache in his back, he did not seem to have been injured. The snow had broken his fall. He saw the crumpled fuselage of his aircraft lying a hundred yards away and began to walk towards it. As he did so, he was puzzled to hear a series of sharp cracks. He still had some thirty yards to go when it dawned on him; the cracks were the whiplash reports of rifle bullets, passing perilously close.

Mathewson threw himself down under cover, taking out his revolver and preparing to shoot it out with the North Korean soldiers who came running towards him, but his three friends overhead had been keeping a watchful eye on him and now they came down to rake the enemy with accurate machine gun fire. For ninety minutes, while Mathewson kept his head down, relays of American and Australian fighters flew patrols over him, diving down to shoot up anyone who made a move in his direction. Eventually, a little Stinson L-5 rescue aircraft arrived and landed close by, its pilot braving intense small arms fire to take Mathewson on board.

Mathewson was soon flying again, but after his seventh combat mission over North Korea severe pains in his upper back forced him to visit the flight surgeon. The doctor took one astonished look at the X-ray plates and gave orders that would keep Mathewson in a hospital bed for fourteen months. He had been flying with a broken neck.

On 15 February 1951 Detachment F was called upon to carry out its most difficult and dangerous task so far, supplying badly needed medical supplies to elements of the US 2nd Division, surrounded by enemy forces in a pocket at Chipyong-ni, some 20 miles east of Seoul. The operation was flown by six H-5s and continued until dark, each helicopter making three sorties into the pocket. On the homeward run, they brought out a total of thirty wounded men. The operation resumed at first light the next day, but with only four helicopters; the other two were unserviceable. The weather grew steadily worse during the morning, with squalls of snow sweeping over the frozen rice fields, and by mid-afternoon the helicopters were battling their way through snowstorms and winds of up to 40 knots. They nevertheless succeeded in evacuating a further twenty-two casualties before nightfall.

In March 1951, the H-5s rescued six out of seven F-80 pilots of the 35th Fighter Group brought down over enemy territory. By this time the Detachment was badly overworked, its task becoming ever more demanding as the air war over Korea intensified. Apart from rescuing downed aircrew, the helicopters were heavily in demand for casualty evacuation – a major headache, for the H-5 could carry only two passengers in addition to its two-man crew, which often meant several sorties a day into the battle area – as well as a number of other sundry tasks. The position improved somewhat after 23 March 1951, when two experimental Sikorsky YH-19 (S-55) helicopters arrived in the theatre to be evaluated under combat conditions. Within 24 hours they had joined the H-5s in evacuating injured and wounded American paratroops from a dropping zone at Munsan-ni, just south of the 38th Parallel, where the 187th Airborne RCT had been dropped in an attempt to cut off Chinese forces falling back on Kaesong. The drop was part of Operation Ripper, the Allied drive north to the Han river, and was the second largest airborne operation of the Korean War, with eighty C-119s and fifty-five C-46s of the 314th Group and 437th Wing employed. Before the end of the day the C-119s had dropped 2011 paratroops and 204 tons of supplies, while 1436 paratroops and sixteen tons of equipment were dropped by the C-46s. The first helicopters arrived over the DZ only fifteen minutes after the first paratroops had landed, and almost immediately they came under heavy mortar and machine gun fire. Two H-5s were hit by small arms fire on the first sortie, but the damage was not serious and they did not have to be withdrawn from the operation. By nightfall on 25 March, after two days of daylight operations, the H-5s and YH-19s had made seventy-seven sorties into the Munsan-ni sector and evacuated 148 paratroops, of whom forty-eight were jump casualties.

In June 1951 the helicopter unit was redesignated Detachment 1, 3rd Air Rescue Squadron, and was split up into four separate flights, one serving the 8055th Mobile Surgical Army Hospital (MASH), another attached to the US 25th Division Command Post close to the centre of the UN battle line, a third earmarked for use by UN truce negotiators, and the fourth on permanent standby at Seoul, once again in UN hands and the Detachment's headquarters. Later in the year two H-5s were moved to the islands of Paengyong-do and Cho-do, from where they made a number of highly effective rescues from Korean waters.

With air combats developing at altitudes of over 30,000 feet, it was inevitable that the Korean War should see new records set for high-altitude parachute escapes. An air battle fought on 29 August, 1951, between Gloster Meteor Mk 8s of No 77 Squadron, Royal Australian Air Force, and Chinese MiG-15s saw the highest recorded baleout to date. On this day, eight Meteors were detailed to escort B-29s and another eight to carry out a diversionary sweep north of Sinanju. At 11.20 the latter flight, led by Squadron Leader Wilson, spotted six MiGs at 40,000 feet over Chongju, 5,000 feet higher than themselves. Keeping the enemy in sight Wilson manoeuvred his formation up-sun, but as he did so two more MiGs appeared a few thousand feet below. Wilson decided to attack and went into a dive followed by his number two, Flying Officer Woodroffe. As the two Meteors levelled out, however, Woodroffe's aircraft suddenly flicked into a spin (an unpleasant tendency of the Meteor 8, caused by the effects of compressibility, if the aircraft exceeded 0.8M at altitude) and dropped away; the pilot managed to recover several thousand feet lower down, but now Wilson had no one to cover his tail. As he began his approach to attack, a MiG jumped him out of the sun, unnoticed in the 30-degree blind spot caused by the dural structure at the rear of the Meteor's cockpit. The first warning Wilson had of the danger was when cannon shells passed over his wing; he immediately put his aircraft into a maximum-rate turn in a bid to shake off his pursuer. He was rescued by Flight

Gloster Meteor F.Mk.8s of No 77 Squadron RAAF in their blast-proof revetments at Kimpo Air base, Korea. (RAAF)

Lieutenant Cedric Wilson and Flying Officer Ken Blight, who spotted his predicament and drove the MiG away – but not before cannon shells had shot away Sqn Ldr Wilson's port aileron and punched a three-foot hole in his port wing, puncturing a fuel tank. Despite the damage Wilson reached base safely, touching down at 30 knots above normal landing speed.

Meanwhile, a fierce air battle had developed over Chongju as the other Meteors were hotly engaged by thirty MiGs. The weight of the attack fell on 'Dog' section, led by Flt Lt Geoff Thornton, who saw the MiGs coming down and ordered his section to break as soon as the enemy opened fire. Flying in the number four position was Warrant Officer Ron Guthrie, a veteran of fourteen previous Meteor sorties over Korea, and as he broke hard to port his aircraft was hit by cannon shells aft of the cockpit, destroying his radio equipment. Two of Guthrie's attackers passed in front of him and he got one in his sights, loosing off a burst of 20mm cannon fire, but before he had time to observe any result he came under attack again, and this time the Meteor went out of control.

As the Meteor passed through 38,000 feet in a rolling dive, with the Machmeter showing 0.84, Guthrie ejected. The Martin-Baker seat worked perfectly and Guthrie sat upright in it as it descended through the stratosphere. It was like sitting in an armchair, with the world unfolding at his feet, and the situation might almost have been pleasant had it not been for the fact that he was falling into enemy territory and that his oxygen mask had been ripped away on ejection. Fortunately, it was still attached to the emergency supply and he managed to get it back on, finding to his relief that

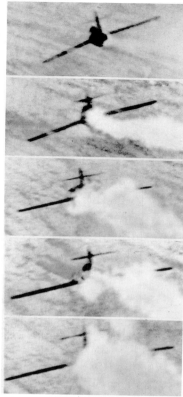

A MiG-15 falls victim to a North American F-86 Sabre's six 0.5 inch machine guns. (USAF)

the oxygen was still flowing.

Guthrie now had a decision to make. The air temperature at that altitude was minus 50 degrees C and he was wearing only a lightweight summer flying suit. If he jettisoned his seat and opened his canopy at this stage, there was would be a very real danger of frostbite. On the other hand, altitude would give him an advantage: he might be able to steer his parachute clear of the North Korean coastline and make a touchdown in the sea, where he would have a good chance of being picked up by friendly forces. He decided to take the risk. Unfastening his harness, he kicked the seat away and pulled the ripcord.

His parachute opened at 35,000 feet. From that height he could see the curvature of the earth, and the whole panorama of the Korean peninsula spread out below him. The air grew warmer as he continued his descent, but now he realised with dismay that a westerly wind was blowing him inland, and that despite his best efforts to control the direction of his parachute he was not going to reach the coast. Twenty-eight minutes after ejecting, having survived the attentions of some enemy troops who fired at him in the latter stages of his descent, he landed in a paddy field and was quickly surrounded. It was the beginning of a two-year captivity. At that time, Guthrie's was the highest ejection on record. He had also experienced the longest parachute descent, and it was the first time that a Martin-Baker seat had saved a pilot's life in combat.

It was soon apparent that the Meteor was no match for the MiG-15, and it was soon reassigned to the ground attack role, which it performed well, leaving the F-86 Sabres to tangle with the MiGs in the stratosphere. Ground

A MiG-15, hit by gunfire from a B-29 bomber, goes down out of control and its pilot bales out. (USAF)

Gun camera sequence shot by an American F-86 Sabre showing a communist pilot ejecting from his crippled MiG-15. The American pilot was Lt Edwin E. Aldrin, Jr, who later became the second man to walk on the moon. (USAF)

A Grumman F9F Panther attacking a target in Korea with rockets. It has also dropped a bomb, which is visible below the puff of white rocket exhaust smoke. (US Navy)

attack work in Korea was difficult and dangerous; quite apart from the nature of the terrain, targets were usually well defended. If an aircraft was hit, the pilot had two choices: either he could bale out into enemy hands, or he could try to gain sufficient height to nurse his crippled aircraft back to friendly territory, where he could either bale out or attempt a crash landing.

Many US Navy pilots narrowly escaped with their lives during the long-running interdiction campaign against enemy transportation. In one instance, a young ensign of Navy Fighter Squadron VF-51, USS *Essex*, was strafing a target near Wonsan when his Grumman F9F Panther jet was badly hit and began to lose height. At about 20 feet off the ground the aircraft struck a pole and lost 3 feet of its starboard wing. Despite this, the pilot nursed the crippled aircraft up to 14,000 feet and took stock of his situation. The undercarriage was jammed in the up position, the rockets were hung up, and the radio was knocked out. The only course of action, under the circumstances, was to bale out over friendly territory, which he did.

Eighteen years later, on 20 July 1969, that fortunate pilot – Neil Armstrong – became the first man to set foot on the moon.

This Panther didn't make it. An F9F plunges into the sea after a failed attempt to touch down on its carrier. The pilot survived. (US Navy)

CHAPTER SEVEN

SUPERSONIC BALEOUT

For 31-year-old George Franklin Smith, Saturday, 26 February 1955 began with a trip to the laundry. It ended with Smith fighting for his life, and assured of a place in aviation history.

George Smith was Inspection Test Pilot with North American Aviation, a job that involved checking out the combat aircraft that rolled off North American's production lines and ensuring that everything was up to scratch before the jets were dispatched to military units. It had been a tough week, with a lot of flying, so on this Saturday morning, with the luxury of a free weekend ahead of him, Smith allowed himself to lie in until 8.30 in his Manhattan Beach apartment. Later, over a light breakfast, he wondered what he was going to do with his free time. He was a bachelor, so there was no one but himself to worry about. Well, he decided, there was no hurry. He would do a few chores first, then make up his mind.

F-100 Super sabres on the flight line at the North American factory, awaiting delivery to the US Air Force. (North American)

At 9.30, he threw his laundry bag into his car and set off to go into town. He dropped off the laundry, picked up some fresh clothing and did a little shopping, and then, on a sudden impulse, decided to drive out to the North American factory at Los Angeles International Airport. He remembered that he had left a test report unfinished the day before, and since the factory was only a five-minute drive from his apartment he thought he might as well compete the paperwork before going home for lunch. That way, he wouldn't have to face the report first thing on Monday morning.

It took him about half an hour to finish the report. Afterwards, he thought he would wander over to the pilots' rest room for a coffee. There he found two of his fellow pilots, Joe Kinkella and namesake Frank Smith, who were taking a break between flights. There was always someone at work during the weekend, keeping the wheels turning.

George chatted with his colleagues for a while, then they left to take up a pair of F-100 Super Sabre fighters and he thought he might as well go home. He was just about to head back to his car when he was stopped by Bob Gallahue, one of the dispatchers whose job it was to supervise the rolling out of new aircraft on to the flight line and turn them over to the company test pilots.

'No 659 is ready to fly,' Gallahue told Smith. 'Do you feel like taking her up before you go?'

The pilot agreed readily. The flight would not take long, perhaps forty-five minutes at the outside, and it was as good a way as any of filling in the rest of the morning.

No 659 was a brand new Super Sabre, fresh out of the factory and waiting to make its maiden flight. Smith signed the appropriate technical log sheets and pulled on a life jacket over his sports shirt and slacks. Because it was only going to be a short trip, he didn't bother with the usual procedure of donning a reinforced nylon flying suit and boots.

Ten minutes later he was sitting at the end of the long runway, carrying out the pre-takeoff checks that by this time were second nature to him. Everything seemed to be in order. The instruments indicated that the big, supersonic fighter's complex systems were working as they should. Only once, as Smith moved the control column to check its action, did the thought flash through the pilot's mind that something was slightly amiss; the stick felt stiffer than normal. On checking his instruments, however, Smith found that the hydraulic pressures in the control system were well within limits, and the stiffness was so barely perceptible that he decided to ignore it.

He called for take-off clearance, cut in the afterburner as the Super Sabre gathered speed down the runway, and soon the fighter was blasting into the sky under the 16,000-pound thrust of its Pratt and Whitney J57 turbojet. Still climbing, Smith turned on a course for the usual test area near San Diego, taking the Super Sabre up to 35,000 feet, high above the dense cloud layer that was slowly creeping in over the coast.

Levelling out, Smith began a straight fast run, pushing the fighter up to

A North American F-100 Super Sabre high over California. (North American)

Mach 1, the speed of sound. At this altitude the Super Sabre was capable of Mach 1.3, or in layman's terms something in the region of 860 miles per hour.

The needle of the Machmeter flickered briefly as it reached and passed Mach unity, the flicker caused by the sonic shock wave braking back over the aircraft's flying surfaces and the pitot tube, the stalk-like protuberance that jutted out from the F-100's nose. It was air pressure, rammed into this tube, that governed the function of both the airspeed indicator and the Machmeter.

Sound waves travel at roughly 12 miles a minute, so thirty seconds after the fighter nosed past the Mach anyone who happened to be out at sea, within a 10-mile swathe below the hurtling aircraft, would hear a sonic boom.

Trouble struck without warning. Abruptly, the fighter began to nose over. Smith immediately pulled back on the stick, fighting to re-trim the aircraft, but it wouldn't budge. He tried again, using all his strength, but it was useless. The dive grew steeper. Still struggling to regain control, Smith called up Los Angeles and reported his predicament. The dive was almost vertical now, and the clouds were leaping up to meet the jet with terrifying speed.

A few miles away, Joe Kinkella was carrying out his own test programme when his attention was caught by Smith's distress call. Looking around, he saw the vapour trail of his friend's Super Sabre spearing downwards toward the cloud layer. Pressing the transmit button, he yelled: 'Bale out, George! Get out of there!'

Smith needed no prompting. With the controls still locked solid and the speed increasing wildly with every passing second, he knew that he had to get out – fast.

He made one last frantic call: 'Controls locked – I'm going straight in!' Then, with his right hand, he pulled up the arm-rest of his seat to jettison the cockpit canopy. The perspex hood flew off with a bang and a terrific blast of air raged into the cockpit with a noise like a long, buffeting explosion. Half stunned, his senses numbed by the howling tornado, Smith instinctively crouched forward in his ejection seat, a move that left him in exactly the wrong position for ejection. Even under the most favourable circumstances, in the correct posture with back straight, pilots who eject often suffer spinal injuries, although these mostly tend to be of a minor nature. Smith, leaning forward to shield himself from the raging airflow, risked very severe injury indeed. Moreover, in the urgency of the moment he forgot to pull his feet back off the rudder pedals and on to the ejection seat footrest. Failure to do so could mean the brutal amputation of both legs below the knees when the seat blasted the pilot clear of the cockpit. Later seats were fitted with special leg-restraining garters which automatically pulled the feet back when the ejection sequence was started.

Smith had no recollection of pulling the ejection seat handle. His last memory was a glimpse of the Machmeter, indicating Mach 1.05. The next instant, the roaring supersonic airflow slammed him unconscious as he was hurled clear of the plunging aircraft.

By the time Smith managed to bale out, the Super Sabre was down to less than 7000 feet, having plummeted down the sky for 4½ miles. Its speed when the pilot ejected was about 1140 feet per second, nearly 780 miles per hour. Smith had got out just in time. There was a delay of approximately four seconds between the seat and pilot leaving the cockpit and the automatic deployment of the parachute after the seat dropped away; if Smith had hesitated for just two seconds more, he would have hit the sea with his parachute unopened.

Below the cloud layer, Los Angeles businessman Art Berkell, lawyer Mel Simon and Simon's fifteen-year-old son Robert were fishing on the twenty-foot cruiser *Balabes,* anchored off Laguna Beach. It had been a miserable morning, with frequent showers of cold rain, and several times they had been on the point of packing up and going home, but they were keen fishermen and each time they had decided to carry on for just a little longer. Their decision was to save George Smith's life.

There was a sudden, terrific explosion and a great fountain of water erupted two hundred yards astern, accompanied by a concussion and a surging wave that nearly capsized the little craft. Their first reaction, on seeing the geyser of water, was that they had strayed into a naval gunnery range. Then young Robert gave a shout, pointing, and they saw a parachute drifting down from the clouds, a limp figure dangling beneath it. Quickly, they started the boat's engine and headed for the area where the parachute looked as if it would enter the water. As they did so, there was the scream of a turbojet and Joe Kinkella's Super Sabre roared overhead. Kinkella had also spotted the parachute and now radioed the information to the company station, call-sign X-Ray Romeo Tango, at Los Angeles. Further away, Frank Smith heard the call and he too streaked towards the scene at top speed.

Smith was in a pitiful state. His clothing was torn to shreds, and his helmet, oxygen mask, shoes and socks had all been ripped away by the fearful blast of air. Blood streamed from cuts on his face and feet. Worse still, about a third of his parachute canopy was torn and useless, and the remainder was only partly deployed.

It was an unexpected gust of wind that saved him. Seconds before he hit the seas, it inflated what as left of his canopy and checked his rapid rate of descent.

Still unconscious, Smith hit the water with a smack. As he was senseless and therefore unable to inflate hs lifejacket, he would have sunk quickly had it not been for yet another coincidence: pockets of air were trapped in his torn flying suit and kept him afloat for the minute or so it took the *Balabes* to reach him.

Even now, Smith's amazing luck continued to hold. During the Second World War, Art Berkell had captained an air-sea rescue launch and had fished no fewer than 275 airmen from the sea. He knew exactly what to do in this kind of emergency. Nevertheless, getting Smith safely aboard the boat was a tough job; the pilot weighed 215 pounds and his clothing was waterlogged, and it needed all their combined strength to haul him over the gunwale.

Berkell knew that they had to get Smith to hospital, and quickly. Apart from his cuts and bruises, the pilot's eyes seemed to be badly damaged. They were horrifying to look at: two brimming pools of red, caused by ruptured blood vessels. While Berkell applied some basic first aid, which contributed greatly to Smith's survival, Mel Simon set course for the coast.

Luckily, two Coast Guard auxiliary cruisers were also at sea off Laguna that morning, practising rescue techniques. The faster of the two, alerted by a radio call, now raced to intercept Simon's boat. Minutes later, the injured pilot was transferred to the cruiser which rushed him to the harbour at Newport Beach, where an ambulance was already standing by to take him to the Hoag Memorial Hospital.

For days, doctors fought to keep Smith alive. His heartbeat was so weak that it was almost unnoticeable, and his blood pressure so low that it was off the chart. The doctors were handicapped by the fact that they had never before treated a man blasted into a supersonic wall of air, and they did not know what internal injuries to look for.

In fact, until this moment the belief had been widely held that it was impossible to survive a supersonic baleout. Only the year before, in October 1954, North American's senior test pilot, George S. Welch – who in December 1941 had achieved fame as one of only a handful of American pilots who had succeeded in getting airborne to oppose the Japanese attack on Pearl Harbor – had been testing the Super Sabre in a dive when the aircraft broke up at 20,000 feet. Welch baled out, but he was fatally injured and died on the way to hospital.

Now George Smith, in a state of deep shock and fighting for his life, had shown that survival was possible. His recovery, however, was slow, and it was small wonder. Within hours of the accident, his face swelled up to the size of a football and turned deep purple in colour. His superficial injuries were much more extensive than had been apparent to the men who rescued him from the water. There were large areas of bruising and laceration on his head, feet, legs, shoulders and back, while his lips, ears and eyelids were bruised and bleeding as a result of fluttering rapidly in the intense airflow. The joints of his knees and arms were loose, too, and as the days went by it was found that his lower intestine and liver had been seriously damaged during the violent buffeting. During the long weeks in hospital, his weight dropped to 150 pounds.

Most of the damage, the doctors calculated, had been caused by the enormous 'g' forces to which Smith had been subjected. Aviation medicine experts worked out that his body had sustained a wind-drag deceleration of 64g when he first ejected, and had then been subjected to 29g for around twenty seconds. The initial terrific force had the effect of increasing his body weight to an incredible 13,760 pounds – some six tons – followed by twenty seconds at 6235 pounds. The weight of every organ in his body had increased correspondingly, and his super-heavy blood had caused severe haemorrhage as it pounded round his body. Adding to the overall damage was the fact that Smith had tumbled uncontrollably between leaving the seat and his parachute deploying, with consequent rapid fluctuations in the 'g' forces he was experiencing and further severe strain on his internal organs.

While Smith was fighting his way back towards recovery, Navy salvage teams were searching for the remains of his Super Sabre. They eventually located it less than a mile offshore, in 134 feet of water. In over a month of salvage operations they succeeded in recovering 90 per cent of the aircraft: tiny fragments of metal that filled fifty barrels. The largest chunk pulled up was the compressed, impacted engine. For weeks, accident investigators pored over the wreckage in a hangar at the North American factory, and finally came up with the theory that the failure of a coupling in the hydraulic system had been at the root of the trouble. Modifications were carried out on all other F-100s; George Smith's traumatic experience had not been in vain.

Smith lay in hospital for seven months while doctors and aviation medicine experts kept him under constant observation. On 23 August 1955 he was once again pronounced physically fit and regained his commercial flying certificate, returning to his old job with North American. His weight increased again, but only as far as 175 pounds. He actually felt a lot fitter for the weight loss, but as he was fond of remarking to people who asked him about his supersonic escape: 'It sure is one hell of a way to slim!'

The North American F-100 Super Sabre

Originally known as the Sabre 45, the F-100 bore little resemblance to its predecessor, the F-86, having a contoured low-drag fuselage, and wings and tail surface swept at an angle of 45 degrees. On 1 November 1951 the USAF awarded a contract for two YF-100A prototypes and 110 F-100A production aircraft; the first prototype flew on 25 May 1953 and exceeded Mach 1 on its maiden flight. The first F100A Super Sabres were delivered to the 479th Fighter Wing at George AFB, California, in September 1954, but were grounded in November following a series of unexplained crashes. It was established that the vertical tail surfaces were too small to maintain control during certain manoeuvres, and so they were redesigned with 27 per cent more area, the wing span also being slightly increased. With these modifications the F-100A began flying operationally again in February 1955 and twenty-two examples were built. The next series production variant was the F-100C, which was capable of carrying out both ground attack and interception missions. First deliveries to the USAF were made in July 1955 and total production was 451, of which 260 went to the Turkish Air Force. The F-100D differed from the F-100C in having an automatic pilot, jettisonable underwing pylons and modified vertical tail surfaces; it was supplied to the USAF Tactical Air Command, Denmark, France and Greece. The TF-100C was a two-seat trainer variant and served as the prototype of the TF-100F, which flew in July 1957. Total production of all Super Sabre variants was 2294, many aircraft serving in Vietnam.

By an odd coincidence, a few days before Smith regained his commercial licence, a second pilot made a successful supersonic escape on the other side of the Atlantic. He was twenty-two-year old Flying Officer Hedley Molland, a fighter pilot with No 263 Squadron, Royal Air Force. Based at Wattisham, in Suffolk, No 263 had recently exchanged its twin-jet Gloster Meteor Mk. 8 jet fighters for more modern swept-wing Hawker Hunter F.Mk.5s, which were capable of exceeding Mach 1 in a shallow dive.

Just after noon on 3 August 1955, Molland and a sergeant pilot named Alan Blow took off in their Hunters and climbed out over the sea. For the next

Hawker Hunter jet fighters in impeccable formation. These are Mk 1s of No 43 Squadron. Three of the aircraft are fitted with ammunition link containers (the bulges under the nose). (MoD RAF)

fifteen minutes the two pilots carried out practice interceptions on each other, filming the results with their camera guns. Then, with Molland tail-chasing Blow's Hunter, they went up to 40,000 feet, where they flew straight and level for a minute before entering a shallow dive.

A few seconds later, the two fighters slipped gently past Mach 1, still over the sea about 4 miles off Felixstowe. Suddenly, Molland noticed that he was gradually overhauling Blow's aircraft, so he eased back the stick to check the dive. At that speed the controls should have been fairly stiff, so Molland was surprised when the stick moved back easily. He was even more surprised, not to say alarmed, when nothing happened and the Hunter continued to dive, the angle growing steeper all the time.

At 30,000 feet, Molland decided to bale out, although not without some misgivings. A glance at the Machmeter showed that it was reading 1.1. Molland had heard about George Smith, and knew something of the injuries the American had sustained. With this in mind, it looked as though his own chances of survival were pretty slim, yet it was better to take the chance than to sit in the cockpit and wait for certain death.

Despite his dire peril, Molland's brain stayed calm. His one main fear was that if he jettisoned the cockpit canopy, the sudden inrush of air would prevent him reaching up to grasp the handle of his ejection seat, so he decided to carry out both actions simultaneously. Gripping the firing handle with his left hand, he pulled the hood jettison handle with his right. The cockpit canopy flew off and the airflow roared in with a noise like an express train, blinding him. He couldn't see anything, but he had managed to keep his grip on the seat firing handle and now he pulled it, bringing the protective blind down over his face and igniting the ejection cartridge.

Molland blacked out as soon as he was blasted into the airflow. He was unconscious for only a few seconds, and when he came to he found himself falling in his seat with the air whistling past him. His Martin-Baker ejection seat was fitted with two drogue parachutes; both had deployed successfully and the seat, with Molland still strapped in it, was falling in an upright position and decelerating gradually. A few months earlier, George Smith's injuries would probably have been fewer if he had enjoyed the benefit of a similar seat, but his Super Sabre was fitted with an American seat which was not equipped with drogues, and consequently tumbled wildly.

Molland had baled out at an altitude of about 25,000 feet. With an indicated Mach number of 1.1, that meant he had ejected at a true airspeed of around 760 miles per hour. In getting out at 25,000 feet he was a lot more fortunate than Smith, for the atmosphere at that altitude was far less dense and its 'brick wall' effect on his hurtling body much less damaging.

As he dropped seawards in his seat, Molland was relieved to discover that he could see again. Then, with a sudden shock, he realised that his left arm seemed to have disappeared. Groping frantically for it, he found that it had been caught by the airflow and dragged around the back of the seat with such force that the bone had broken between shoulder and elbow. He hauled it in

Ground crew remove the Martin-Baker ejection seat from a Hawker Hunter for routine servicing. (MoD RAF)

with his right hand and tucked it into the seat straps to keep it out of the way. Almost dispassionately, he noticed that his wrist watch had been torn off by the blast, as had his oxygen mask, flying helmet, left shoe and sock. If he had baled out a few thousand feet higher up, he might have perished from oxygen starvation. His face was painful, and he discovered later that one of his straps

had lashed him fiercely, blackening both his eyes and making his nose bleed. Also, he saw that the attachments which held his dinghy to his Mae West lifejacket had come undone.

He reached down and managed to refasten one of the dinghy attachments. As he did so, he saw a splash far below him as his Hunter plunged into the sea. Then, as he passed through 10,000 feet, his seat fell away cleanly and his parachute opened.

He was about 3 miles offshore, but the wind was carrying him out to sea all the time and he remembered with a sudden shock that he could not swim. He would have to rely on his Mae West and dinghy, and as the sea drew nearer he inflated the lifejacket as a precautionary measure. He hit the water a few minutes later and at once found himself in trouble when he became entangled with his parachute shroud lines. He tried to inflate his dinghy, but with only one hand was unable to manage it. His lifejacket kept him on the surface, but he spent an uncomfortable few minutes being dragged along by the billowing canopy, which refused to collapse.

As things turned out, it was the canopy which attracted the attention of the crew of a tug, cruising a few hundred yards away, and guided the vessel to the spot. Molland was picked up within ten minutes and the tug took him to Ipswich, where he was transferred to the Borough General Hospital. Doctors told him that he had a fractured pelvis in addition to his broken arm, but apart from that his injuries were not serious.

Molland had been lucky. Just how lucky, he learned from the tug's crew, who told him cheerfully that they had been towing a target to provide firing practice for some shore batteries. If the pilot had baled out a couple of minutes earlier, he would have landed amid a barrage of shells.

Hawker Hunter

Early in 1946, both Hawker and Supermarine were studying schemes for swept-wing jet fighters. Two specifications were issued by the Ministry of Supply, both calling for experimental aircraft fitted with swept flying surfaces. Both companies submitted proposals in March 1947, the Hawker design being designated P.1052. This aircraft flew in November 1948, and its performance was such that at one point the air staff seriously considered ordering the type into full production to replace the Gloster Meteor. Instead, the design was developed further under Air Ministry Specification F.3/48, the operational requirement calling for a fighter whose primary role would be the interception of high-altitude, high-speed bombers. The fighter was given the designation P.1067. The outbreak of the Korean War, together with fears that it might escalate into a wider conflict, led to the acceleration of combat aircraft re-equipment programmes in both east and west. In Britain, the two new swept-wing fighter types, the Hawker P.1067 – soon to be named the Hunter – and Supermarine's design, the Type 541 Swift, flew in prototype form on 20 July and 1 August 1951 respectively and both types were ordered into 'super-priority' production for RAF Fighter Command. The Hunter F.Mk.1, which entered service early in 1954, suffered from engine surge problems during high-altitude gun firing trials, resulting in some modifications to its Rolls-Royce Avon turbojet, and this – together with increased fuel capacity and provision for underwing tanks – led to the Hunter F4, which gradually replaced the Canadair-built F-86E Sabre (which had been supplied to the RAF as an interim fighter) in the German-based squadrons of the 2nd Tactical Air Force. The Hunter Mks 2 and 5 were variants powered by the Armstrong Siddeley Sapphire engine; it was the Mk 5 that Hedley Molland was flying at the time of his accident. In 1953 Hawker equipped the Hunter with the large 10,000 pound thrust Avon 203 engine, and this variant, designated Hunter F.MK.6, flew for the first time in January 1954. Deliveries began in 1956 and the F6 subsequently equipped 15 squadrons of RAF Fighter Command. The Hunter FGA.9 was a development of the F6 optimised for ground attack, as its designation implies. The Hunter Mks 7, 8, 12, T52, T62, T66, T67 and T69 were all two-seat trainer variants, while the FR.10 was a fighter-reconnaissance version, converted from the F.6. The GA.11 was an operational trainer for the Royal Navy. In a career spanning a quarter of a century the Hunter equipped 30 RAF fighter squadrons, in addition to numerous units of foreign air forces.

CHAPTER EIGHT

THE PILOTS WHO WOULDN'T BALE OUT

At 15,000 feet, the cockpit of the big Boeing KC-97G tanker was pleasantly warm. Apart from the readings shown on an outside air temperature gauge, there was no hint that the crew were separated only by the thickness of the aircraft's skin from blistering, sub-zero cold. Far below, the long shadows of the Arctic night hid the vast wastes of Greenland.

In the distance, beyond the curve of the earth, the ghostly veils of the aurora danced and flickered, but the crew took no notice of them. They were all part of the scene in these latitudes; just one factor in an unreal, alien weather pattern where the ionosphere could suddenly go crazy, radio transmissions be blacked out for minutes on end and compass needles spin wildly.

It was 27 November 1956, and for the crew of the KC-97G this was just another routine training mission. The big Boeing, callsign 'Turmoil Five', was one of six similar aircraft spaced at intervals in the Arctic darkness, orbiting over fixed positions. All of them belonged to the 26th Air Refueling Squadron (ARS), USAF Strategic Air Command, operating out of Thule in Greenland.

In the dangerous years of the mid-1950s, with East-West tension at its height, a new term had come into being: the nuclear deterrent. Twenty-four hours a day, seven days a week, a proportion of Strategic Air Command's mighty bomber fleet patrolled these icy skies, armed with thermonuclear

A Boeing KC-97G flight refuelling tanker of the type flown by Flight Lieutenant Max Barton. (USAF)

weapons and instantly ready to strike at targets deep in the heart of the Soviet Union should the latter launch a surprise attack. The bombers' life blood during those long hours on patrol was JP-4 fuel, thousands of gallons of it, gulped down by their thirsty turbojets. Supplying that fuel was the task of the flying tankers of the 26th ARS, and others like it.

Tonight, the tankers were to rendezvous with Boeing B-52 Stratofortresses, the giant eight-engined jet bombers which were the latest additions to Strategic Air Command's fleet. It was a task that called for very precise flying on the part of both bomber and tanker pilots; positioning the two aircraft for the transfer of fuel was a tricky process, for there was a considerable speed margin between the B-52 and the much slower, piston-engined KC-97G.

Nevertheless, every member of the tanker crew knew his job intimately, and they all had faith in the skill of their aircraft captain, even though he was a relative newcomer to the flight refuelling business. He was Flight Lieutenant Max Barton of the RAF, an Englishman on a two-year exchange tour with the US Air Force. Barton had joined the RAF in 1944 at the age of eighteen and had originally trained as a navigator, flying in Lancaster bombers. Demobilised at the end of the war, he had taken a course in aeronautical engineering, after which he had gone to work in the research and development department of A.V. Roe and Company, the British aircraft manufacturers who at that time were designing the radical new delta-winged jet bomber which was to enter service with the RAF as the Avro Vulcan. Flying was in his blood, however, and in 1950 the RAF had accepted him back for pilot training. He had graduated from the flying training school at RAF Feltwell, Norfolk, with honours, receiving all three of the major trophies awarded to the best student at the end of each course.

All the other members of the KC-97G's crew were Americans. Beside Barton, in the right-hand seat, sat Second Lieutenant 'Nick' Nichols, the co-pilot, and behind them, at their stations on the roomy flight deck, were the navigator, radio operator and flight engineer. Separated from the rest of the crew, surrounded by fuel gauges and pipes in a position near the tail of the aircraft, was the refuelling boom operator.

Barton brought the KC-97G out of its orbit, flying straight and level at 15,000 feet on a predetermined heading. The navigator, Captain Jim Sullivan, was watching the 'blip' of the approaching B-52 on his radar screen, and passed a steady flow of information about its progress to Barton, who was in radio contact with the bomber. Now, as the B-52 came up astern and below, closing steadily, the boom operator, Staff Sergeant Painter, crept down into a blister beneath the tanker's rear fuselage. Lying on his stomach in this position, he extended the tanker's long refuelling boom and took over the radio link with the B-52 pilot, guiding the latter into position and manoeuvring the boom until it locked into place in a hatch on top of the fuselage, behind the cockpit.

Locked together, the two aircraft sped through the freezing night. From the

KC-97G's great reservoirs, fuel passed through the boom into the B-52's tanks at the rate of 600 gallons per minute. The radio operator, Staff Sergeant Morris Carmon, had earlier left his place on the flight deck and now stood in the rear fuselage compartment just forward of Painter's position; with the aid of a flashlight he kept a watchful eye on the spot where the tanker's intricate 'plumbing' merged with the main four-inch fuel pipe. It was Carmon's job, at this stage in the mission, to detect and rectify any major leaks that might develop as the JP-4 fuel passed through the pipe under high pressure.

It was cold and gloomy in this remote section of the aircraft, with nothing but the throb of the KC-97G's four powerful Pratt & Whitney radial engines for company, but the refuelling task was already more than half complete and Carmon would soon be back in the warmth of his radio position. Then, as these thoughts were running through his mind, he suddenly heard a noise that made his blood freeze. Loud above the beat of the engines came a powerful hissing sound, like a punctured tyre. An instant later, Carmon gagged as strong JP-4 fumes penetrated his face mask.

Painter smelt it too, and knew what had happened even before Carmon sounded the alarm. Both men turned their oxygen fully on and Painter alerted the pilot, at the same time shutting off the flow of fuel and retracting the boom. He waved it slowly from side to side in front of the B-52 pilot, signalling that contact was to remain broken, and the big bomber moved quickly away.

Up on the flight deck, Barton rapidly assessed the situation and set emergency procedures in motion. With highly explosive fuel leaking rapidly into the fuselage, the slightest spark could turn the big aircraft into a ball of fire, so the first task was to switch off the main electricity supply. Barton quickly selected a power setting of 19 inches manifold pressure and set the engine revolutions to 1900 rpm. Then he ordered the flight engineer to throw the master switch.

Instantly, every control and instrument that depended on the KC-97G's main electrical supply ceased to function. Radio and intercom went dead, and the needles of most of the instruments on Barton's panel dropped to zero. Reduced panel lighting and three instruments – the artificial horizon, turn and slip indicator and directional gyro – were kept going by the emergency power supply. The heating also failed and Barton no longer had any control over the pitch of the aircraft's propellers. This, together with the fact that the flaps were also inoperative, would make a landing extremely tricky. Navigation back to base would also be a problem, for Jim Sullivan's radar and radio aids were useless.

Barton had taken the precaution of depressurising the cabin, and now he ordered the crew to jettison the hatches in the hope that the noxious fumes might blow away. A howling, icy gale blasted into the fuselage as the hatches whirled away.

Jim Sullivan, using dead reckoning, quickly worked out a rough course for

Thule, which was some 250 miles away, and passed his calculations to Barton. The latter turned the tanker on to the new heading and descended cautiously to 10,000 feet. Meanwhile, in the rear of the aircraft, Painter and Carmon were already up to their ankles in JP-4 as they searched for the leak. The hiss of escaping fuel was deafening, and despite their oxygen masks the men were sickened by the stench.

It was Painter who found the leak – an X-shaped rupture about three inches across in one of the pipes. Through it, fuel was spurting into the fuselage at 50 gallons a minute. Instantly, Painter knew that there was no possibility of repairing the damage. Followed by Carmon, he went forward to report to the aircraft captain. With the intercom useless, conversation was difficult; the men had to remove their oxygen masks and shout a few words at one another, then replace their masks quickly before the fumes overwhelmed them.

Barton made a quick reappraisal of the situation. There were already hundreds of gallons of fuel sloshing about in the fuselage, pouring from the KC-97G's upper tanks, and the aircraft's main electrical connection box was practically submerged. Any spark would certainly cause a devastating explosion. Barton was literally flying a bomb. To make matters worse, the weight of loose fuel was beginning to affect the trim of the aircraft; anything other than the gentlest of control movements would cause the JP-4 to rush either fore and aft and make the KC-97G critically unstable. There was another worry, too. The loss of electrical power meant that the de-icing equipment no longer worked, and the risk of airframe and engine icing grew with every minute the tanker remained in the air.

Barton knew that some attempt had to be made to drain the growing volume of fuel from the aircraft, so he ordered three of the crew members to go aft and jettison the rear exit door in the hope that the JP-4 would flow out. They waded through the freezing, stinking liquid only to find that fuel had seeped round the edges of the door and frozen solid. Not daring to use axes in case they caused a lethal spark, they spent several minutes trying vainly to dislodge the door. It was hopeless. They came forward again, exhausted with the cold and their exertions, their senses reeling with the fumes.

Jim Sullivan, working hard at his plotting table with the aid of a flashlight, was continually passing course corrections to the pilot. Barton, although finding that controlling the aircraft needed all his concentration, was now fairly certain that he could reach Thule. One by one, he called the other members of the crew up to the cockpit and gave them a choice; either they could stay with the aircraft as he rode it down for a dangerous landing, or they could take to their parachutes when he flew over the airfield. Baling out into the darkness over frozen, rocky ground would be risky, but by now the men were glad of any chance to escape the suffocating fumes. They all elected to jump except Nichols, the co-pilot, who elected to stay with Barton.

The KC-97G droned on through the night, the men on the flight deck straining their eyes for the glimmer of light that was their base. After an hour, a shout of relief went up as they caught sight of a faint glow, a long way off and to the right, reflected from a thin layer of cloud. It had to be Thule; there were no other lights for hundreds of miles.

Barton's problems, however, were only just beginning. The next task was to lower the aircraft's undercarriage, and without electrics it had to be wound down manually. The whole thing had to be done by operating a series of cranks and levers all in strict order, and in the darkness it was several minutes before the job was finished. Even now, the pilot had no way of knowing whether the undercarriage was locked in position, for the loss of the electrics meant that the three green lights that normally showed in his instrument panel were absent.

Barton ordered the crew to put on their parachute packs and began a slow descent to 5000 feet, turning gently towards the airfield. He reduced the airspeed to 160 miles per hour; without flaps, he dared go no slower. Very precisely, he lined up with Thule's main runway and then indicated to the men in the fuselage that it was time to jump. One by one, with difficulty because of the slipstream, they made their exits into the darkness.

Now only Barton and Nichols were left, and it seemed very lonely in the large, vibrating cockpit. Barton brought the tanker round in a wide turn, circling the airfield to approach the runway for a landing. He had to get everything right first time, for any sudden increase in power or abrupt change of trim would cause the tons of fuel to shift and result in disaster.

Suddenly, the panel lighting went out. The emergency electrical supply was exhausted, and now he was left only with the airspeed indicator and turn and slip indicator, neither of which depended on electrics. Barton was glad that Nichols had stayed behind, for he was able to read the last two working instruments with the aid of a pocket torch which the co-pilot focused on them.

The KC-97G thundered down through the night towards Thule's main runway. Although the temperature in the cockpit was far below freezing, sweat poured down the faces of both men. Barton had never attempted a landing in a heavily-laden aircraft with no flaps, and his mind was working overtime. He had no idea of the tanker's all-up weight, a crucial factor when working out the best approach speed. At best, he could only compromise. He decided to maintain 160 mph all the way down the approach, reducing to 145mph as they crossed the runway threshold. In layman's terms, that meant that the big aircraft would be touching down as fast as a jet fighter. Although the runway was 10,000 feet long, he realised that he might not be able to stop the tanker before it careered off the far end. He also knew that if he held the nose too high on the final approach, the tons of fuel in the rear would swirl backwards and send the aircraft out of control – but he would have to raise the nose to bleed off some speed.

As 'Turmoil Five' continued her long, flat approach towards the runway threshold, rescue services on the airfield, alerted by the parachuting crew members, were going into action. Sirens wailed as ambulances and fire tenders raced around the perimeter track and took station beside the runway.

In the aircraft's cockpit, Barton had eyes only for the lights ahead as Nichols called out the airspeed by the light of his torch. Vaguely, the pilot was aware of the darkened landscape, sweeping past beneath the tanker's wings. He realised that he was a little high, so he shouted to Nichols to reduce the power a fraction. The co-pilot complied instantly, easing back the throttles, and the aircraft sank a couple of hundred feet.

The runway threshold was coming up fast now, and Barton – very, very gently – began to apply backward pressure to the control column. Beside him, Nichols continued to call out the speed. She was floating, her main undercarriage skimming the surface of the runway. Barton raised the nose a fraction higher and a moment later felt a heavy jolt as the wheels finally touched. He knew that behind him, the mass of JP-4 would be flowing towards the rear of the fuselage and that he had to get the nose down, for if the tail scraped against the concrete the resulting friction would blow them to kingdom come. Firmly, he shoved the control column forward.

Nothing happened. The runway raced beneath them at 200 feet per second and still the nose remained obstinately in the air. Barton went on pushing, his arms rigid and the sweat standing out in beads on his brow.

If they were not to finish up as a pile of burning wreckage among the rocks at the far end of the runway, he had to use the brakes. But the speed was still 100mph, and the KC-97G's handling notes forbade the use of brakes above 60 mph. To apply them now risked having the undercarriage collapse, and if that happened it would be all over. In a fraction of a second, Barton weighed up the alternatives and made his decision. As the tanker careered down the icy runway like a juggernaut, leaving the racing fire tenders and ambulances far behind, he trod gently, just for a split second, on the mainwheel brake pedals. It was the merest touch, but it was enough. The wheels locked a fraction and the nose began to come down, slowly and reluctantly. A second later, the nosewheel's comforting rumble sounded on the runway.

Burton was able to use the brakes fully now, and gradually the big aircraft lost its momentum. It finally came to a stop threequarters of the way down the runway. For a few moments Barton and Nichols sat unmoving, scarcely able to believe that they had got down safely. Then Nichols let out his pent-up breath with an explosive gasp and the two men relaxed, grinning at each other.

Even now, the danger was not over. As they left their seats, Barton noticed fuel seeping under the forward escape hatch. Not daring to risk any friction, the two men decided to make their exit through an emergency hatch in the flight deck. Someone on the ground tossed them a rope and they slid down it.

To his immense relief, Barton learned that all his crew had landed safely. Then, as he turned to inspect the aircraft, he realised how lucky he and Nichols had been. Fuel was pouring out of every crevice and wisps of smoke still curled from the mainwheels, the result of the heavy braking during the last few hundred yards of the landing run. Fortunately, no fuel had come into contact with the hot undercarriage units.

On 13 July, 1957, Major General Walter Sweeney, Commanding the United States Eighth Air Force, presented Flight Lieutenant Max Barton with the American Distinguished Flying Cross for outstanding bravery in the air.

The Boeing KC-97G

The KC-97G tanker variant of the C-97 transport, the major production version with a run of 592 (out of a total of 888 military C/KC-97s), was developed to support Strategic Air Command's B-47 Stratojet strategic bomber force, with twenty tankers assigned to every SAC bomber wing. Normal interior equipment provided for ninety-six equipped troops or sixty-nine stretcher cases, without the need to remove transfer tanks and the boom operator's station. Tests with the 'Flying Boom' fuel transfer equipment on KC-97As were followed by the production KC-97E, KC-97F and KC-97G. The last KC-97 modification, the KC-97L, was fitted with J47-GE25A booster jet pods in place of the original long-range underwing tanks. The pods were taken from the KC-97's predecessor in the flying tanker role, the Boeing KB-50, and gave the KC-97L a much-needed speed and altitude boost to enable it to operate more effectively with its receiver aircraft, the Boeing B-47 Stratojet. The KC-97G also acted as a stop-gap tanker for the Boeing B-52 force until the Boeing KC-135 jet tanker (developed from the Boeing 707 airliner) was deployed.

Just under a year after Max Barton's exploit, on 3 October 1957, Flight Lieutenant Jack Pembridge, a Canberra B.6 pilot with No 139 Squadron RAF, was also faced with an emergency that involved a fuel spillage.

During the Second World War, No 139 Squadron, then equipped with de Havilland Mosquitoes, had specialised in target marking, and in the mid-1950s it performed a similar role with its Canberra jet bombers, which regularly deployed from their usual base at Binbrook, Lincolnshire, to Idris in Libya, from where they carried out practice attacks on bombing ranges in the Libyan desert. So it was that, at 1826 hours on 3 October 1957, Pembridge's Canberra, serial number WJ769, lifted away from Idris's runway and headed out into the desert night. In addition to the pilot, the aircraft carried two other crew members: Flying Officer Tony Brown, the navigator, and Flying Officer George Gale, who was acting as observer. It was their second practice bombing sortie of the day.

As the Canberra climbed away from Idris, there was nothing to indicate that anything was amiss. But unknown to the crew, a small amount of fuel had seeped into the port wing from one of the main tanks, just outboard of the Avon turbojet. It flashed into flame at some point during the climb.

At about 4000 feet, Pembridge noticed a strange flickering light, just

English Electric Canberra B.6 bombers in formation. (British Aerospace)

inboard of the port wing-tip fuel tank. Although his engine instruments gave no indication of any trouble, Pembridge quickly assessed the situation, realised that the only explanation for the flickering light must be a fire, and sent out a Mayday call, informing Idris that he was returning with a fire in the port engine. It was just five minutes since take-off.

Pembridge throttled back and closed the port high-pressure fuel cock, causing the port engine to flame out, and selected full air brakes as he turned back to Idris. The airspeed quickly dropped to 200 knots, and the fire warning light suddenly came on. Pembridge pressed the fire extinguisher button and retracted the airbrakes. The glow from the wing continued to increase and was now accompanied by a series of bangs from the port wing. The fire had eaten through the integral tank fuel transfer line and fuel was seeping steadily from the severed line, feeding the blaze.

Pembridge jettisoned the tip tanks. The fire was now beginning to affect the port aileron and control became difficult. Pembridge found that he had to apply full starboard aileron to prevent the Canberra rolling to port, and a good deal of rudder was needed to prevent yaw.

The Canberra was now down to 3000 feet and descending towards Idris at 200 knots. Suddenly, the fire warning light went out and the glow decreased. Pembridge thought the emergency might be over. He throttled back the starboard engine and the speed dropped to 190 knots, but even with full starboard aileron and right rudder the aircraft was still tending to roll to port. The pilot selected full starboard aileron trim and some right rudder trim, but found by experiment that he could not open up his starboard engine much without having to dive the aircraft to maintain lateral control. Pembridge now considered making a high-speed landing at nearby Wheelus Air Base, which was under American control.

His hopes were abruptly dashed by an explosion in the port wing, followed by a burst of bright light and a streamer of flame that reached back as far as the tail. Pembridge saw at once that the skin of the wing's upper and lower surfaces had burnt through, creating an extremely dangerous situation. Port aileron control had gone completely now, and the situation was getting steadily worse. It was time to go.

Pembridge gave the order to abandon the aircraft, and a few moments later the navigator ejected safely. The observer, Flying Officer Gale, did not have an ejection seat and had to make his exit through a hatch in the fuselage side, which he did successfully after something of a struggle against the slipstream and his parachute harness, which at one point became snagged on a seat adjustment lever. Luckily, Pembridge saw what had happened, tugged the harness free and literally booted Gale out through the open door.

Pembridge was now faced with a dilemma. Ahead of him was the town of Tripoli, and he decided to delay his own ejection until he was clear of the populated area. Once he was certain that he was over open country he prepared to eject, but then he made another rapid appraisal of the situation and decided that, as he as now about 750 feet above ground level, he might as well make an emergency landing on Idris airfield's runway 36. By the time he turned on to final approach the port wing was well ablaze, and was probably only seconds away from collapsing.

Pembridge selected wheels down, but the undercarriage failed to respond and the Canberra crash-landed on its belly, careering down the runway in a cloud of dust and a screech of tortured metal, hotly pursued by a fire tender. It eventually came to a stop and its dazed pilot unfastened his harness and climbed out through the open hatch, turning to watch as the crew of a fire tender sprayed foam on the blaze and on the starboard engine, which was still running because the high-pressure cock had jammed.

All in all, it had been a close shave. Canberra B.6 WJ769 was a write-off, but its crew had escaped with their lives. That was the important thing.

* * * *

In protecting an English village, Colonel Wendell J. Kelley, USAF, made the supreme sacrifice. In 1963, Colonel Kelley was deputy commander of the 20th Tactical Fighter Wing (TFW), then flying F-100 Super Sabres from Wethersfield in Essex. Kelley, who was forty-three, lived off-base with his wife and three children in the nearby village of Gosfield, where he was deeply involved in a number of local activities to do with youngsters and had played a big part in raising funds for a new village playing field.

On the morning of 23 January, 1963, Kelley took off from Wethersfield in a two-seat F-100F on an instrument training sortie over southern England. The pilot he was checking out was twenty-five-year-old First Lieutenant Paul Briggs.

Halfway into the sortie, when they were at 30,000 feet north of London, there was an explosion in the F-100's engine, followed by a loss of power. The aircraft was still under control, so Kelley put out an emergency call and received a radar steer to the Blackwater Estuary, where he jettisoned the Super Sabre's underwing fuel tanks. Anglia Control then gave him a heading for Wethersfield and he turned towards base, the aircraft descending slowly under reduced engine power. Anglia control brought him down through the cloud layer to position his aircraft for a straight-in approach to Wethersfield's main runway.

Both pilots knew that as long as they had a margin of power available they would be able to reach the airfield, but while they were still in cloud the worst happened: there was another explosion and the engine flamed out. Kelley tried to relight it, but it had seized solid.

The Super Sabre broke through the cloud base at 6000 feet. At 4500 feet it still had six or seven miles to go, and there was now no possibility of reaching the runway; with a dead engine the heavy aircraft would be at zero altitude in 5 miles or less. While Briggs kept the F-100 on its glide path, Kelley made further attempts to relight the engine, but without success. Calmly, he told Wethersfield's approach controller that he intended to turn the aircraft towards a clear spot where both pilots could eject.

On the ground, eyewitnesses saw the Super Sabre alter course several times to take it clear of the little town of Halstead and the scattered villages that lay in its path. With the altitude down to 1500 feet Kelley ordered Briggs to eject. The younger pilot did so successfully, but Kelley remained at the controls as the aircraft, becoming increasingly unstable, descended towards Gosfield, where Kelley had made his home. At 200 miles per hour the jet plunged into a nearby field and exploded. Kelley had made no attempt to eject.

A few days later, more than 250 villagers braved the worst snowdrifts they could remember to attend a memorial service for Colonel Kelley in Wethersfield. They were convinced that the pilot had deliberately sacrificed his own chances of survival by staying at the controls to ensure that the plunging aircraft missed the homes of the people who had become his friends.

The same kind of skill and professionalism had earlier been displayed by two more 20th TFW pilots, on that occasion with a happier outcome. On 23 October, 1957, Lieutenants Ray Krasovich and Billy Ray of the 55th Fighter-Bomber Squadron, which had recently converted to F-100s, took off from Wethersfield on a two-ship training sortie over the North Sea. As they rejoined formation after practising some individual manoeuvres, Ray, momentarily blinded by the sun, collided with Krasovich's Super sabre, damaging its rear fuselage and buckling its tail, while his own aircraft lost two feet of its nose, together with the pitot tube. Without this his airspeed indicator ceased to function, which would present a critical and possibly fatal problem during the approach to land. Nevertheless, both aircraft were still handling adequately, and Krasovich decided to accompany Ray's F-100 right down to the runway threshold so that the other pilot could match his approach speed.

That nose out in front there looked awful odd, Ray said later, but Kraz made a good job of bringing me in. I could hear the GCA (Ground Controlled Approach) instructions through my headphones and always, just when I would normally have glanced at the clock, Kraz broke in with the airspeed. We broke cloud. I was right up level with Kraz's wing and we were both nicely lined up with the runway. He took me right down to approach speed and up to the end of the runway. Few pilots need their ASI after that – they just feel the aircraft down.

With Ray safely over the runway threshold and within yards of touchdown, Krasovich broke away and climbed back into the circuit. He knew that it would be dangerous to have two damaged aircraft careering down the runway at the same time, and he had also noticed that his own aircraft's damaged tail was causing handling problems at low speed. Accordingly, he flew around for a while to get the feel of the F-100 at low speeds before making his own approach to land, which he accomplished successfully.

Super Sabre pilots were the first to admit that without power the aircraft's gliding qualities were akin to those of a brick. One aircraft, though, was worse: the McDonnell F-101 Voodoo, and it was in an F-101 that Captain Jack E. Shephard of the 91st Tactical Fighter Squadron, 81st Tactical Fighter Wing, found himself presented with a very unenviable situation during a sortie from Bentwaters, Suffolk, in October 1960.

Shephard was returning to base after a two-hour practice bombing sortie over France. The weather was bad and he positioned himself over the North Sea for a GCA (Ground Controlled Approach), turning left towards the coast and the instrument runway at his home airfield. At 1800 feet, with everything going smoothly and the voice of the GCA controller holding the Voodoo nicely on the glide path, Shephard closed the throttles to lose speed prior to lowering the undercarriage. With the landing gear down and locked he went to push open the twin throttle levers again, and it was then that his problems began. The levers refused to budge.

The Voodoo was down to 1400 feet now, and if its sink rate remained unchecked it would crash on the Suffolk coast in less than sixty seconds. At first Shephard thought that the throttle levers had in fact moved but that there must be some problem with the fuel system, so more valuable seconds were wasted while he tried switching tanks, and by the time he realised that the levers themselves were causing the trouble his aircraft was descending through 1000 feet.

Shephard considered ejecting, but the prospect of plunging into the icy North Sea was far from appealing. Moreover, he was appalled by the thought

A McDonnell F-101 Voodoo in flight. (McDonnell Douglas)

of the Voodoo plummeting down somewhere on the quiet coastline, perhaps causing civilian casualties. Releasing his safety harness, he managed to get his left foot behind the throttle levers and shoved with all his strength. He was fighting for his own life now; with his harness undone he could not eject, and he would not have enough time to strap himself in again before his aircraft reached too low an altitude.

Over the radio, the GCA controller's voice was becoming more and more urgent as he saw the Voodoo's blip sinking lower on his radar screen, but Shephard was too busy trying to move the throttle levers to find time for the radio. Still pushing desperately hard with his foot, he finally felt one of the levers budge a little – not much, but enough to restore some vital engine power. Slowly, the heavy fighter-bomber began to climb back on to the glide path.

Shephard dared not take his foot off the lever, because as soon as he did so it snapped back into the closed position again, and the Voodoo went down the glide slope in a kind of porpoising motion, its engine power surging when he pushed the throttle lever and falling away again as soon as he relaxed the pressure. Fortunately, because both its engines were close to the fuselage centreline, the Voodoo suffered no serious asymmetric flying problems, so Shephard had no need to take his foot off the throttle lever to operate the rudder pedals.

The Voodoo broke cloud a mile short of the runway, and Shephard saw at once that he was too low. Power came on as he shoved the throttle lever again, but it was not enough, and as a last resort he cut in the afterburner, gaining additional thrust to take him over the last few hundred yards. As the runway threshold passed below him he at last moved his aching foot from the lever and the aircraft sank to the concrete as the power died away. The brake parachute popped out and the Voodoo rolled to a stop undamaged, thanks to a very fine feat of airmanship.

The McDonnell F-101 Voodoo

In 1951, the USAF briefly resurrected an earlier long range escort fighter requirement as a result of the combat losses suffered in Korea by Strategic Air Command's B-29s, and McDonnell used its abandoned XF-88 design as the basis for a completely new aircraft, lengthening the fuselage to accommodate two Pratt & Whitney J57-P-13 engines, giving it a top speed of over 1000 mph and a ceiling of 52,000 feet, and increased fuel tankage. In its new guise, it became the F-101A Voodoo. The prototype flew on 29 December 1954, and although Strategic Air Command had long since abandoned the long-range escort fighter idea, the programme was taken over by Tactical Air Command, which saw the F-101 as a potential replacement for the Northrop F-89 Scorpion all-weather interceptor. The aircraft went into production as the F-101A, powered by two Pratt & Whitney J57-P-13 turbojets, and the seventy-five examples built equipped three squadrons of TAC. The next Voodoo variant, the two-seat F-101B, equipped sixteen squadrons of Air Defense Command, and production ran to 359 aircraft. This version also equipped three Canadian air defence squadrons as the CF-101B, and formed a very important component of Canada's air defences; it replaced the very advanced Avro Canada CF-105 Arrow, which was cancelled on grounds of economy. The RCAF's CF-105Bs were normally held at five-minute readiness when on air defence alert.

Most interceptions of Soviet reconnaissance aircraft were made by No 416 Squadron at Chatham, Ontario, by nature of its geographical location. The F-101C was a single-seat fighter-bomber version for TAC, entering service with the 523rd Tactical Fighter Squadron of the 27th Fighter Bomber Wing in May 1957. It equipped nine squadrons, but its operational career was relatively short-lived, as it was replaced by more modern combat types in the early 1960s. F-101C Voodoos were based at RAF Bentwaters, Suffolk, England with the 81st Tactical Fighter Wing from 1958 to 1965, when the type was replaced by the F-4C Phantom. The Voodoo replaced the 81st TFW's F-84F Thunderstreaks, which were transferred to the Federal German Luftwaffe.

CHAPTER NINE

COLD WAR CASUALTIES

As tension increased between East and West in the years following the Second World War, high-altitude reconnaissance flights over the Soviet Bloc and China by American and British aircraft became almost routine, as did their attempted interception by fighter aircraft and missiles. Many more flights were made around the periphery of the USSR as NATO 'ferret' aircraft probed the secrets of Russia's air defences, gathering electronic information that would have meant the difference between life and death for the USAF and RAF bomber crews tasked with the nuclear annihilation of key targets in the Soviet Union. A number of these aircraft fell victim to fighters or missiles, the facts surrounding their true fate covered up for many years after the event. And in some cases, the fate of aircrew, believed to have baled out of stricken reconnaissance aircraft, remains a mystery to this day. What is not a mystery is that, in the ten-year period between 1950 and 1960, seventy-five USAF and US Navy personnel lost their lives while flying these highly dangerous missions.

By the end of the Korean War, the component squadrons of the 55th Strategic Reconnaissance Wing, which was the USAF Strategic Air Command unit primarily responsible for electronic intelligence-gathering missions, had exchanged its ageing Boeing B-29s for the Boeing RB-50. At Yokota, the 55th TRW's Detachment Two, consisting of the 343rd Strategic Reconnaissance Squadron, used the RB-50G model, which was configured specifically for the electronic intelligence (ELINT) role. (Other variants, the RB-50B and RB-50D, were configured for photo-mapping and photographic reconnaissance).

Early in the morning of 29 July, 1953, an RB-50G (serial number 47145) of the 343rd SRS took off from Yokota to carry out an ELINT mission in the Vladivostok area, a frequent target for such sorties. The aircraft carried six electronic intelligence specialists (known as Ravens)as well as its usual flight crew of eleven. At about 06.15, the RB-50G was at 20,000 feet, some 26 miles off Cape Povorotny to the south-east of Vladivostok, when it was attacked by MiG-15s and two of its engines knocked out. The aircraft's starboard wing caught fire and began to disintegrate, collapsing and breaking away moments after the pilot, Captain Stanley O'Kelley, ordered the crew to bale out.

Twenty hours later an American destroyer picked up Captain John E. Roche, the co-pilot and sole survivor of the seventeen-man crew. Roche stated that he had been accompanied in the water for a time by O'Kelley, but that the two men had lost contact and the pilot had presumably drowned.Three bodies were later recovered after being washed ashore on the coast of Japan; thirteen crewmen were listed as missing. In the years that followed, however, there were persistent reports that other crew members had also baled out and had been captured by the Russians; it was certain that Soviet patrol craft had combed the area – which was shrouded in mist at the time – because Roche had heard them. He also claimed to have heard the voices of fellow crew members, calling for help.

The US Air Force continued to insist that the aircraft (which it referred to as a B-50, not an RB-50) had been on a routine navigational training flight and that it had been shot down over international waters. The US State Department presented the Russians with a claim for $2,785,492.94, which included replacement of the aircraft and compensation for the families of the dead airmen. The Russians at once replied with a counter-claim for $1,861,450 in respect of a Russian Ilyushin Il-12 transport aircraft, shot down by an American F-86 Sabre on the last day of the war in Korea. The Il-12 had been flying from Lu-Shun in China to Vladivostok, taking a short cut across a narrow strip of North Korean territory that jutted into Manchuria, where its wreckage fell. All twenty-one on board – presumably Soviet military personnel who had been taking an active part in the war – were killed.

Was the shooting down of the RB-50 a reprisal for the destruction of the Il-12? That will never be known, but it seems certain that the Russians were lying in wait for the reconnaissance aircraft. The presence of Soviet naval craft at the exact place where the interception took place is evidence enough, and it seems likely that their crews had orders to rescue any surviving Americans and bring them ashore for interrogation. According to some sources, that is exactly what happened. In 1991, with the cold war over, the Russians and Americans agreed to establish a joint commission called Task Force Russia, its object being to investigate the fate of any Americans who might have fallen into Soviet hands after the end of the Second World War. The opening of this door enabled relatives of some missing airmen to visit Russia and make enquiries of their own; one of them was Bruce Sanderson, whose father, Lieutenant Warren J. Sanderson, was one of the RB-50 aircrew unaccounted for.

When Sanderson visited Moscow in the autumn of 1992 he met a former Soviet intelligence officer turned military historian called Gavril Korotkov, who was adamant that six airmen – including Lt Sanderson – were captured and interrogated by a KGB counter-espionage unit. Refusing to co-operate, the Americans were classed as spies and sent to Gadhala prison camp in south-central Siberia. If the story is true – and it is highly unlikely that it will ever be verified – it is improbable that any of the men would have survived their captivity.

The loss of the RB-50 led to future ELINT missions being provided with a fighter escort wherever possible, an arrangement that certainly saved an RB-50 on 22 January 1954 when it was attacked by MiGs over the Yellow Sea. The attackers were beaten off by sixteen F-86F Sabres, which shot one of them down. Two more American reconnaissance aircraft, however, were lost in the north-western Pacific in 1954. On 4 September, a P2V Neptune of Patrol Squadron VP-19 was attacked by two MiG-15s off the Siberian coast and forced to ditch in the Sea of Japan. On this occasion most of the crew were lucky; although one went down with the aircraft, nine were rescued. But only three days later, an RB-29 was shot down into the Sea of Japan off Hokkaido with the loss of thirteen crew. The toll was mounting, and not only reconnaissance aircraft were the victims. On 23 July 1954, a Cathay Pacific airliner was shot down by Chinese fighters off Hainan Island, and three days later two Douglas AD Skyraiders of Air Group 5 from the carrier USS *Philippine Sea*, searching for survivors, were attacked by a pair of Lavochkin La-7s or La-9s. The US Navy pilots turned the tables and destroyed both Chinese aircraft. On 17 April 1955 the Russian fighters scored their first success against the new Boeing RB-47E Stratojet when a 55th SRW aircraft, on detachment to Japan, was shot down off Kamchatka, possibly by MiG-17s. Since 1954 the *Fresco*, to give the MiG 17 its NATO code-name, had been replacing the MiG-15 in the Soviet Air Force's far eastern fighter regiments, and its presence – as was the case in the west – stripped the RB-47 of the relative immunity it had enjoyed so far.

On the morning of 2 September, 1958, a four-engined Lockheed C-130 Hercules of the United States Air Force took off from the NATO air base at Incirlik, in southern Turkey, and set course north-westwards. The Hercules was attached to the 7406th Combat Support Squadron, which was normally

The Lockheed P2V Neptune was a victim of the Cold War, one being shot down by MiG-15s in 1954. (Lockheed)

Another victim of the Cold War was the Lockheed EC-121 surveillance aircraft, one being shot down by North Korean fighters in 1969. All thirty-one crew perished. (Lockheed)

based at Rhein-Main Air Base near Frankfurt, Germany. The Hercules, which had first entered service with the USAF's Military Air Transport Service in December 1956, was an amazingly versatile aircraft, able to carry a wide variety of cargoes and to operate, if necessary, out of rough airstrips anywhere in the world. It was still to be the workhorse of America's air transport fleet, and the principal tactical transport aircraft of many other nations, forty years later.

On that September day in 1958, however, the C-130 cruising over the mountains of Turkey was not one of the USAF's transport fleet. It was an EC-130, it was operated by the US National Security Agency, and it was on a signals intelligence gathering mission. Its spacious fuselage was packed with advanced electronic equipment and it carried a crew of seventeen men, thirteen of whom were radio and radar specialists. Their mission was to intercept and identify signals from the network of Soviet radar stations to the north of the Black Sea and in Armenia and Georgia; signals that would tell them not only what type of radar was being used, but also reveal its range and other information.

The first leg of the EC-130's flight took it high over the 12,000 foot peaks of the Canik mountains. Ninety minutes and 350 miles out from Incirlik the aircraft was over Trabzon, on the north coast of Turkey, and the pilot, Captain Paul E. Duncan, turned right through 90 degrees and headed for Lake Van, 250 miles away in the south-east corner of Turkey. This new heading took the Hercules parallel with the border of Soviet Armenia, which was about 100 miles away off the aircraft's port beam.

The Hercules never reached Lake Van, and an extensive search for it all over eastern Turkey turned up no clues as to its fate. On 6 September, after considerable discussion, the American Embassies in Moscow and Tehran formally asked the Russians and Iranians if the aircraft had come down in their territory, having strayed over the border by accident; both governments denied all knowledge of it. Then, on 12 September, the Soviet Foreign Ministry stated that the wreckage of an American military aircraft had been discovered near the village of Sassnaken in Soviet Armenia, some 35 miles north of the town of Yerevan, and that six badly mutilated bodies had been recovered. The Russians claimed that the EC-130 had deliberately violated their air space, an allegation which – in view of the circumstances surrounding the EC-130's mission – the Americans naturally denied. The next day, in fact, the American chargé d'affaires in Moscow handed a note to the Soviet Foreign Ministry, alleging that the Hercules had been intercepted by Soviet fighters close to the Turkish-Armenian border, that the American pilot had obeyed the fighters' instructions to follow them eastwards, but that his aircraft had been deliberately destroyed shortly afterwards. It was claimed that eye-witnesses on the Turkish side of the border had seen the Hercules turn towards the east; soon afterwards, they had heard an explosion and had seen a column of smoke rising from a point within Soviet territory.

These allegations were flatly denied by the Russians. Then the Americans played their trump card. Monitoring stations in Turkey, they stated, had made a tape recording from a Soviet radio frequency of what appeared to be R/T chatter between four Russian pilots. The date and time of the transmission tallied exactly with that of the EC-130's disappearance, and the

A Lockheed C-130 Hercules, similar to the one shot down by Soviet fighters in 1958.
(Lockheed)

translated text of the Russians' conversation, as released by the USAF, was as follows:

I see the target, to the right.
I see the target.
Roger.
The target is a big one.
Attack by... (transmission garbled)
Roger.
The target is a four-engined transport.
Target speed is three-zero-zero. I am going along with it. It is turning towards the fence.

At this point the transmission became garbled, the voices of the Russian pilots high-pitched and excited. Then:

The target is burning.
There's a hit.
The target is burning, 582.
281, are you attacking?
Yes, yes, I... (transmission garbled)
The target is burning... the tail assembly is falling off the target. 582, can you see me? I am in front of the target.
Look, look at him, he will not get away, he is already going down.
Yes, he is going down. I will finish him off, boys, I will finish him off on this run. The target has lost control. It is going down.
The target has turned over... aha, you see, it is falling.
All right, form up, head for home.
The target started burning after my third pass...

The Americans made no admission that the Hercules had penetrated Soviet air space, but there was no longer any doubt that this had happened when, on 24 September, the Russians – who had dismissed the tape recording as a crude fabrication – returned the remains of six crew members, only four of whom could be identified. No other bodies were handed over, despite repeated American requests. The US Deputy Under-Secretary of State, Robert Murphy, subsequently issued a statement to the effect that:

...the American pilot, as a result of signals transmitted by radio beacons in Soviet Georgia and Armenia, had probably made a navigational error which resulted in his unintentionally crossing the Soviet border.

The statement then went on to claim that the Hercules had then been fired on by Soviet aircraft and destroyed.

In fact, the statement implied that the EC-130 had been deliberately lured over the Soviet border by false radio signals and then shot down. If Captain Paul Duncan had been relying on his radio aids rather than on visual navigation – which was likely, since significant landmarks in the rugged terrain of north-east Turkey were few, and in any case the C-130 was over cloud during the last leg of its flight – then the Russians could have jammed the Lake Van radio beacon transmissions and superimposed their own. A few degrees' deviation from its planned course would have been enough to take the Hercules over Soviet territory. It is likely that Captain Duncan only realised his mistake when the Russian fighters appeared, and that he immediately turned west towards the frontier; but by then it was too late.

Then, in October 1958, came another extraordinary twist to what was already a bizarre story. *Sovietskaya Aviatsiya,* the daily newspaper of the Soviet Air Force, published an article purporting to describe an 'air exercise' in which four Soviet jet fighters shot down an 'intruding enemy aircraft'. Significantly, the callsigns of two of the fighters mentioned in the article were identical with those on the American tape; courses and altitudes were also similar. According to the article, the four fighters were scrambled from separate airfields with an interval of several minutes between each pair and were guided to the target by two fighter controllers, Major Kulikov and Captain Romanyuta. The callsigns of the leading fighters (which were unidentified, but probably MiG-17s) were 582 and 281. They were flown by Lieutenants Lopatkov and Gavrilov. The article stated that by the time the second pair of fighters arrived on the scene, their take-off having been delayed by a sandstorm, Lopatkov and Gavrilov had already made three passes at the target and set it on fire. The work of destruction was completed by the other two pilots, Lieutenants Kucheryayev and Ivanov. For years afterwards, there was speculation that some of the American crew members had survived and had been interrogated and then imprisoned by the Russians, but in 1995, following the end of the Cold War, the incident was investigated by a joint US-Russian commission, which investigated the crash site and interviewed witnesses. An excavation turned up human bone fragments at the scene, and no evidence was produced to suggest that there had been any survivors. As to the theory that the Hercules had been deliberately lured over the border, this remained a possibility; just a few weeks earlier, on 27 June 1958, a USAF C-118 transport had crashed inside Soviet territory in the same area.

* * * *

In April 1960, America's Central Intelligence Agency (CIA) received information that the Russians were developing what appeared to be a very advanced missile site near Sverdlovsk, and a Lockheed U-2 high altitude reconnaissance aircraft was detailed to photograph it, together with the missile test centre at Tyuratam and the air and naval bases at Archangelsk and Murmansk. The aircraft selected for the mission was a U-2B (serial 56-6693). The U-2B was a modified U-2A, one of seven fitted with the 15,800 pound thrust Pratt & Whitney J75-P-13A engine; range, payload and airframe fatigue life were all extended, and the aircraft was internally strengthened to accept the higher thrust and increased weight of the new engine.

At the end of April 56-6693 was deployed from its usual base at Incirlik,

Turkey, to Peshawar in Pakistan. Most overflights took place from this location, as traffic from Incirlik was heavily monitored by the Russians. This particular U-2 was not a favourite aircraft with its pilots, who had encountered fuel transfer problems while changing from one tank to another in the air. Nevertheless, it was the only U-2 that could be spared for the mission, so at 0626 local time on the morning of 1 May 1960 it took off from Peshawar and climbed out over northern Afghanistan on the first leg of a nine-hour, 2800-mile flight over the Soviet Union that would terminate at nightfall on the NATO air base of Bodo, in northern Norway. It was the first time that a U-2 mission had been planned to fly across the full breadth of the Soviet Union; it was also the first U-2 overflight to take place on communism's traditional day of celebration. The U-2's pilot was a civilian employee of the CIA. His name was Francis Gary Powers, a former USAF pilot who had been recruited by the CIA.

By the time Powers' U-2 crossed into Soviet territory it was flying at an altitude of 68,000 feet. Powers went up another couple of thousand feet, levelled out and switched over to the automatic pilot, noting that the outside air temperature was minus 60 degrees C. Below the aircraft stretched an unbroken bank of cloud, not of particular significance from the reconnaissance point of view at this stage of the flight, for there was nothing much of interest on the surface. When the cloud layer finally ended the pilot found himself more or less on track, south-east of the Aral Sea. Looking down, Powers picked out a condensation trail, arrow-straight across the dark earth and on a reciprocal heading to his own. The aircraft at its head was travelling very fast, possibly at supersonic speed, but it was a long way below and it quickly vanished. A few minutes later another contrail appeared, this time travelling in the same direction as the U-2, but this aircraft too remained far below and Powers eventually lost it.

Baikonur Cosmodrome – the space centre from which, a year later, Yuri Gagarin would blast off to become the first man in orbit – lay on the U-2's track, and although it was not a primary target on the U-2's itinerary it had been decided to include it anyway, as information returned by earlier U-2 flights had proved disappointing. Powers therefore rolled his cameras as he passed over Baikonur before flying on towards Chelyabinsk. The clouds had dispersed completely now, and the snow-capped Ural Mountains were clearly visible, running like a great jagged scar from north to south, cutting through green landscape on either side.

Suddenly, the U-2's nose pitched sharply upwards in a dangerous porpoising motion; it was a vicious trait that all U-2 pilots had learned to anticipate and cope with. Powers quickly disengaged the autopilot and took over manual control, trimming the aircraft for level flight before engaging the autopilot again. The U-2 flew on for about ten minutes and then the nose pitched up again, leaving Powers no choice but to revert to manual control. The fact that he would have to pilot the aircraft manually for the rest of the sortie was by no means a disaster, but it would add considerably to his workload, and he would need all his concentration for the task of monitoring the U-2's reconnaissance systems.

At this point, Powers knew that he would have been quite justified in aborting the mission and turning back, for CIA U-2 pilots were briefed to take such action if anything at all went wrong with the programmed flight. By this time, however, Powers was about 1300 miles deep into Russia and the weather conditions ahead of him were perfect. He decided to press on.

The U-2's next objective was Sverdlovsk, an important industrial centre which was of special interest to US Intelligence because of some curious domed structures, believed to be missile silos, which were reported to be under construction in the vicinity. So far, no U-2 flight had been made over the area. From Sverdlovsk, Powers was briefed to continue to Plesetsk, another missile test centre in the north. Thirty miles south of Sverdlovsk, the pilot made a turn to the left and settled down on a new heading that would take him over the strange installations and the south-west suburb of the town. He had now been airborne for four hours.

As he ran in towards his target, Powers detected an airfield which was not marked on his map, and he logged its position carefully. At that moment, he sensed rather than heard a dull explosion and a vivid orange glare enveloped his aircraft, which lurched violently. The U-2 had in fact been near-missed by an SA-2 *Guideline* surface-to-air missile, one of a salvo of fourteen launched at the high-flying aircraft. Powers was unlucky in that the battery had only recently been established near Sverdlovsk.

It seemed an age, Powers wrote later, before the orange light died away. The U-2's right wing began to sink and he moved the control column over to the left, levelling the aircraft again. Then the U-2's nose dropped, and this time the controls failed to respond. An instant later, a fearful vibration shook the aircraft as both wings tore away. The weight of the engine dragged the tail down and Powers found himself lying on his back. The fuselage began to spin and the 'g' forces pinned him to his seat. The U-2's cockpit was small, the pilot sitting with his legs stretched out in a kind of tunnel beneath the instrument panel. The layout was much the same as that of a high-performance glider, but it meant that before he could eject, the U-2 pilot had to move his seat back on its rails and pull his legs clear of the panel.

Powers pulled the lever that moved the seat, but it refused to budge. Quite simply, this meant that if he attempted to eject now, he would lose both legs a few inches above the knee as he left the cockpit. The only other alternative was to bale out in the orthodox manner. A glance at the altimeter showed him that the U-2, still spinning wildly, was already below 35,000 feet and falling at an alarming rate. He pulled the canopy jettison handle, and almost instantly the faceplate of his pressure helmet frosted over. He unfastened his seat harness, then remembered that he was supposed to activate the U-2's destruct mechanism. If he had ejected this would have happened automatically, but now he had to throw a red-painted switch on the starboard side of the cockpit. He groped for it, unable to see because of his iced-up faceplate, but failed to locate it and decided to concentrate all his efforts on saving himself. He tried to lever himself out of the cockpit, but something pulled him up sharply and there was a moment of panic before he remembered that he had not unclipped his oxygen lead. He tore it free, and a moment later he and the tumbling fuselage parted company.

Powers' parachute opened automatically at 15,000 feet and he landed in a ploughed field close to a Russian village. The rest is history. His subsequent interrogation and trial made worldwide headlines, and the U-2 incident effectively wrecked a major East-West summit conference which was scheduled to be held in Paris a fortnight later. Powers himself was sentenced to ten years' imprisonment in the Soviet Union, but after serving two years he was exchanged for the Russian spy Colonel Rudolf Abel.

Powers was killed in 1977 in the crash of a helicopter that he flew for a Los Angeles television station. While in 1998 declassified Cold War documents revealed that Powers' mission was a joint operation by the CIA and the Air Force, it was not until 1 May, 2000, the fortieth anniversary of the U-2 incident, that the U.S. government posthumously awarded his family the medals denied to Powers while he was alive. Powers' family accepted a Distinguished Flying Cross, Department of Defense Prisoner of War Medal and National Defense Service Medal during a ceremony at Beale Air Force Base in Northern California.

As if to underline their determination to put an end to the Americans' clandestine reconnaissance missions, on 1 July 1960, exactly two months after the Powers incident, the Russians destroyed a Boeing RB-47H over the Barent Sea, north of Murmansk.

The RB-47H belonged to the 343rd Strategic Reconnaissance Squadron, 55th Strategic Reconnaissance Wing, based at Forbes Air Force Base, Kansas, and was temporarily deployed to RAF Brize Norton in Oxfordshire, which was used by Strategic Air Command as a base for B-47 Stratojets on temporary duty deployments to the United Kingdom. The aircraft was crewed by Major Willard Palm, aircraft commander; Captain Freeman Bruce Olmstead, pilot; Captain John McKone, navigator; and three signals specialists: Major Eugene Posa, Captain Dean Phillips and Captain Oscar Goforth, the latter flying his first (and, as things tragically turned out, only) only operational mission. In the RB-47H the specialist signals operators – known popularly 'Crows', although officially called Ravens – were crammed into a compartment only 4 feet high, forcing them to move about on their knees. All three Ravens had to cram themselves into the cockpit before take-off, then crawl down into the compartment, where they sat facing aft, strapped into ejection seats and with solid banks of equipment – scopes, analysers, receivers, recorders and controls – in front and on one side. Raven One was the commander and sat in the right forward corner of the compartment. As well as the banks of equipment in front of him and on his left, there was an array of video, digital and analogue recorders along the wall to his right and behind him. Ravens Two and Three sat side by side at the rear

The Lockheed U-2 achieved notoriety with the shooting down of Francis Powers on 1 May 1960. (Lockheed)

of the compartment, with just enough room between their seats for someone to squeeze through.

The planned route of the flight took the RB-47H northward from England over the North Sea and Norwegian Sea, passing the northern tip of Norway and then turning east to fly over the Barents Sea, following a track over international waters some 50 miles from the Kola Peninsula. As the RB-47H was conducting its reconnaissance mission, a Soviet MiG-19 fighter of the Murmansk-based 206th Air Division shadowed it at a distance, a procedure that was routine. The MiG then turned towards the RB-47H on an intercept course, but passed about 3 miles behind it.

Having flown the length of the Kola Peninsula, still keeping well out over international waters, Captain Olmstead was about to turn on to a reciprocal heading when the MiG-19 suddenly popped up about 40 feet off the RB-47H's starboard wing. The reconnaissance aircraft was at 30,000 feet and maintaining a speed of 425 knots. As Olmstead put the aircraft into a left-handed turn, the MiG-19 broke right, towards the Kola shoreline, then turned back towards the RB-47H and the MiG pilot, Captain Vasily Polyakov, opened fire. The MiG's 23mm cannon shells smashed into the RB-47H's left wing, engines and fuselage, causing the aircraft to enter a spin from which Major Palm and Captain Olmstead were able to recover. Then Polyakov came in for a second attack, and this time the damage he inflicted was so severe that the aircraft became uncontrollable and the order to bale out was given. It was

1800 hours, local time.

Major Palm, together with Captains Olmstead and McKone, all succeeded in ejecting from the stricken aircraft; what happened to the three signals specialists is not known, but it is possible that they had been killed by the MiG-19's gunfire. The other three crewmen descended into the Barents Sea, where Major Palm died of exposure in the freezing water. Olmstead and McKone managed to climb into their rubber life rafts and were picked up by a Soviet fishing vessel after more than six hours.

Within days, Olmstead and McKone were sent to the Lubyanka prison in Moscow and held in separate cells while undergoing interrogation. The airmen were not tortured but were interrogated at length on an almost daily basis. After a while, the Russians permitted a certain amount of correspondence with family members. Throughout the Americans' captivity, their interrogators constantly attempted to persuade the men to indicate regret for the mission and to agree that the United States should cease similar reconnaissance missions.

On 24 January 1961, after almost seven months as prisoners, Olmstead and McKone were released, never having been brought to trial. They never confessed to any wrongdoing and the Soviet espionage case was essentially groundless so the Soviets absolved them of any 'criminal responsibility'. Major Palm's body was returned to the United States about a month after the RB-47H was shot down and buried with full military honours in Arlington National Cemetery, Washington, DC. The bodies of the three signals specialists were never found.

CHAPTER TEN

SOME SURVIVED

In some multi-seat combat aircraft types designed since 1945, only the pilot (or pilots) have had the benefit of ejection seats, other crew members having to abandon the aircraft by conventional means in an emergency. The fact was not so important in the days when bomber aircraft were designed to penetrate enemy defences at high level, because it gave the pilot time to retain control while the rest of the crew jumped before he saved himself, but in the early 1960s low-level operations became the only means of penetrating hostile radar and missile defences, and crew members suddenly found themselves with only seconds in which to get out of a crippled aircraft. This means, simply, that there have been circumstances when a pilot has been unable to climb high enough for other crew members to bale out with any real hope of survival, or to make a controlled crash landing. Under those circumstances, pilots have had to make one of the most terrible of all decisions: whether to eject and save themselves or die with the rest of the crew.

Just such a dilemma, albeit under different circumstances, faced a Royal Navy pilot, Lieutenant Allan Tarver, in 1966.

In May 1966, the aircraft carrier HMS *Ark Royal* was diverted to the east coast of Africa to take part in what was known as the 'oil watch', patrolling the seas off the port of Beira to intercept any tankers carrying oil for the rebel regime in Rhodesia, which had made its unilateral declaration of independence from Britain in the previous November. It was an exacting task, for the area to be searched was twice the size of the British Isles. *Ark Royal's* predecessor on the 'oil watch', HMS *Eagle*, had been on station off Beira for seventy-one days, her aircraft flying over a thousand sorties in that time and her helicopters a further thousand.

The oil-watch flying was not without its risks. The carrier was the only base in the area; there was no diversion airfield available in the event of an emergency. With flying going on at a fairly intensive rate, the occasional emergency was inevitable – such as that which confronted Allan Tarver, a Sea Vixen pilot with No 890 Squadron, on the morning of 10 May 1966.

Tarver was heading back to the carrier at the end of a patrol when several things happened all at once. The port engine flamed out, the electrical system packed in completely, and the instruments indicated that fuel was escaping from the Vixen's tanks at an alarming rate. Tarver immediately called up the Ark Royal, and was advised that a tanker aircraft – a Supermarine Scimitar – had just been catapulted off and was on its way to rendezvous with the Vixen, which was losing height rapidly.

At 15,000 feet, with the *Ark Royal* still 40 miles away, Tarver spotted the

A de Havilland Sea Vixen about to engage the arrester wire on the carrier HMS Hermes. (MoD Navy)

Scimitar approaching from ten o'clock. The Scimitar pilot, Lieutenant Robin Munro-Davies, manoeuvred his aircraft into position above and ahead of the Vixen; from the latter's cockpit, Tarver saw the drogue stream towards him from the tanker. Five times, he tried to make contact with the Vixen's refuelling probe, but by now the heavy aircraft had become unstable and unwieldy and it was impossible to keep it steady enough. Suddenly, the whine of the Vixen's one remaining engine died away as the fuel tanks ran dry and the aircraft started to go down rapidly. The pilot could now see the carrier on the horizon; there was no hope of reaching her, but at least he could stretch the glide for as long as possible before he and his observer, Lieutenant John Stutchbury, were forced to eject. The closer they were to the *Ark Royal*, the better their chances of being picked up quickly.

The de Havilland Sea Vixen, however, was not designed to glide. Powered by two Rolls-Royce Avon turbojets, with a wing span of 51 feet, a length of over 55 feet and a loaded weight of sixteen and a half tons, it was designed to strike hard and fast at speeds of over 600 mph. The Vixen, in fact, glided like a brick.

At 6000 feet, Tarver ordered the observer to eject. Out of the corner of his eye he saw Stutchbury reach up, grasp the firing handle of his ejection seat, and jerk the blind down over his face.

Nothing happened. Over the intercom, Tarver yelled at the observer to try to bale out manually while he held the aircraft as steady as possible. It was not easy. The observer in the Sea Vixen had a pretty uncomfortable position, his seat buried in the starboard side of the fuselage so that his head was just about level with the pilot's backside. It was a tight enough squeeze for a man of average build; but for John Stutchbury, six feet tall with unusually broad shoulders, it was dreadfully cramped. There was no cockpit canopy over the observer, just a hatch in the top of the fuselage; this should have blasted clear when he pulled the seat handle, but it had not.

Stutchbury now pushed the hatch aside and through the perspex of his canopy Tarver saw it whirl away in the slipstream. A second later, Stutchbury's head and shoulders emerged – and stuck fast in the opening. By this time the Vixen was down to 3000 feet. Tarver shoved the stick hard over, hoping that Stutchbury would fall clear as the aircraft rolled over on its back, but the observer still hung there, buffeted by the 200-knot slipstream.

Again Tarver rolled the aircraft, still with no effect. There was just one more chance. He lowered the flaps, reducing the airspeed to 130 knots. The force of the airflow was much less now, and this might just enable the observer to struggle clear. For an instant, it looked as though the plan would work. More of Stutchbury's body slid through the hatch until the observer was lying flat along the top of the fuselage, but something still seemed to be holding him in the cockpit. Tarver reached down into the observer's compartment, his hand groping for Stutchbury's feet. With all his strength, he fought to push his friend clear, but it was no use; the observer now seemed to be unconscious.

There was nothing more that Tarver could do. Even if Stutchbury got clear of the aircraft now, his parachute would not have time to open. The altimeter showed 400 feet and the Vixen was wallowing on the edge of a stall.

Circling overhead in his Scimitar, Lieutenant Munro-Davies saw the Vixen enter a sudden roll to port. When the aircraft was at about sixty degrees, a black shape hurtled from the cockpit: it was the pilot's ejection seat. That was all Munro-Davies saw before the whole scene dissolved in a fountain of spray as the Vixen hit the water. The Scimitar pilot reported that Tarver could not possibly have survived.

But Tarver was still very much alive. His parachute had only partially deployed and he had been stunned by the impact when he hit the sea, but he was able to claw his way from under the silken folds of the canopy and inflate his rubber liferaft. Twenty minutes later, he was picked up by a Wessex helicopter from the *Ark Royal*. His only injury was a strained muscle in his back. For his courage in staying with the aircraft to try to save his friend's life, almost sacrificing his own chance of survival in so doing, he was later awarded the George Medal.

Sometimes, a potentially disastrous situation was saved by quick thinking and instant reactions. One such occasion was in 1967, when Flight Lieutenant Godfrey Ledwidge and his navigator, Flight Lieutenant John Steward, were flying a Canberra B(I)8 of No 3 Squadron RAF on a training mission from their base at Geilenkirchen in West Germany. They had completed a practice bombing run and were recovering to base at 500 feet when they suddenly

Canberra B(I)8s over Germany. The B(I)8 could carry the Red Beard tactical nuclear bomb. (MoD RAF)

encountered serious trouble. Ledwidge turned right, in response to a course correction from his navigator, then moved the control column to bring the Canberra back to level flight again. Nothing happened: the ailerons were jammed solid at an angle of about thirty degrees.

Over the intercom, Steward heard the pilot's warning shout: 'Stand by for some 'g'.' Thinking that they were taking evasive action to avoid another aircraft, for the low-level air space over West Germany was heavily congested by military training flights, Steward braced himself. Then Ledwidge called again, breathlessly: 'Stand by for a lot of negative 'g'. I think we've lost an aileron!'

The seating in the Canberra B(I)8, designed for interdiction operations with either conventional or nuclear weapons, was rather similar to that of the naval

Sea Vixen, with the pilot seated under a transparent cockpit canopy raised above the port side of the nose and the navigator buried in the fuselage beside him, his head level with the pilot's knees. In the Canberra, however, the navigator had no ejection seat; in an emergency, he had to make his exit through a hatch in the fuselage side. When this was jettisoned, a windbreak popped out, shielding him from the airflow as he jumped.

Ledwidge knew at once that Steward would have no hope of getting out at this height, so he applied full power and hauled back the control column in a desperate attempt to gain a few thousand feet. The Canberra immediately entered a roll, which the pilot managed to slow down by using the rudder and juggling with the engine power, but he was unable to prevent the aircraft going over on its back. As it went upside down the nose dropped, so Ledwidge pushed the control column hard forward and speeded up the roll by again using the rudder.

The nose came up agonisingly slowly, and now Ledwidge eased the control column fully back. Beneath them, the ground flashed by only feet away. If the pilot had not speeded up the roll he and his navigator would now be dead, the Canberra a mass of scattered wreckage.

Still rolling, with the pilot applying full rudder one way or the other to speed up or slow down the rate of roll, the Canberra gyrated up to 8000 feet. Although it was under full power, it was sometimes dangerously close to its stalling speed as it whirled across the sky in its crazy aerobatic manoeuvre.

Luckily for navigator Flt Lt John Steward, the Canberra was an extremely agile aircraft. This B(I)8 is seen inverted after rolling out of a bomb-delivery manoeuvre. (MoD RAF)

This photograph shows the escape hatch in the starboard side of the Canberra, through which John Steward had to make his exit. (Bill Swettenham)

Meanwhile, the negative 'g' forces had been playing havoc with the unfortunate navigator, who, having undone his seat harness in expectation of making a rapid exit, had been lifted forcefully out of his seat and buffeted painfully against the roof before falling on to the floor. With considerable difficulty, he retrieved his parachute pack – a chest type – and clipped it on to his harness. Then, reconnecting the intercom lead, which had come loose when he parted company with his seat, he asked Ledwidge if it was okay to jettison the door.

'Yes,' the pilot replied, 'but don't go yet.'

The hatch flew away and a quick check satisfied Steward that the windbreak had popped out. Through the open door, he could see a crazy roundabout of sky and earth. There was no time to feel sick.

With the Canberra's altimeter showing 8000 feet, the speed fell away to only 150 knots as the aircraft wallowed out of another roll. Ledwidge knew that it was going to stall: it was now or never. As the aircraft came the right way up, he yelled: 'Okay – go now!'

Steward disconnected his intercom lead and dived into space. He felt a rush of air, followed by a jolt as his parachute opened. Then he was drifting earthwards, his ears throbbing with the roar of the Canberra's engines as it whirled away.

As soon as he saw that Steward had got out safely, Ledwidge lowered his seat to the position for ejection and pulled the face blind. The seat banged out, separating from the pilot automatically. Both men made a safe landing. Later, Ledwidge's courage in remaining with the crippled aircraft to enable his navigator to escape brought him the award of the Air Force Cross.

Another aircraft with crew escape problems was the Avro Vulcan, the big delta-winged bomber which entered RAF squadron service in 1957 and which, for the next twelve years, formed the backbone of Britain's nuclear deterrent force until that role was taken over by the Royal Navy's Polaris submarines from 1968. In a Vulcan (and also in the RAF's two other V-bombers, the

This photograph shows how rear crew members had to compose themselves in order to make their exit from the Vickers Valiant. (MoD RAF)

Vickers Valiant and Handley Page Victor) the pilot and co-pilot had ejection seats; the other three crew members – two navigators and an air electronics officer – sat facing rearwards at their consoles and had to bale out manually.

This deficiency was highlighted in dramatic fashion at the very start of the Vulcan's career. On 9 September 1956, one of the first two Vulcan B.1s scheduled for delivery to the RAF took off from Boscombe Down on the first leg of a publicity flight to New Zealand via Aden, Singapore and Melbourne. The following month, while approaching to land in low cloud and rain at London Airport at the very end of what had been a triumphant tour, it struck the ground short of the runway and rose into the air again, but was so damaged as to be uncontrollable and crashed. The pilot, Squadron Leader Howard, and the co-pilot, Air Marshal Sir Harry Broadhurst – at that time Air Officer Commanding RAF Bomber Command – escaped by using their ejection seats after making futile attempts to regain control, but the two navigators, the air electronics officer and an Avro representative in the rear of the crew compartment lost their lives.

Another instance where the rear crew might have been saved if they had been equipped with ejection seats occurred on 30 January 1968, when Vulcan B.2 XM604, captained by Flight Lieutenant Peter Tait, took off from RAF Cottesmore on a routine high-level sortie. Soon after take-off the bomb bay temperature was found to be increasing, so Tait decided to abandon the sortie and return to base with the intention of burning off fuel in the circuit. He made one circuit, then the co-pilot made another on the Instrument Landing System (ILS), and on the overshoot Tait took over control and initiated a left turn to avoid an unseen contact ahead. At this point there was a sudden explosion followed by vibration so intense that Tait found it impossible to read his instruments. (It was later established that a fire in number two engine had led to turbine disc separation and the disc had smashed into the bomb bay, severely damaging the flying controls).

The Vulcan's port wing started to drop; Tait took corrective action but was unable to level the wings, so he ordered the rear crew to get out. With the help of the co-pilot, Flying Officer Mike Gillett, he continued his efforts to level the wings by using trim, rudder and throttles in an attempt to gain a few precious extra seconds for the men in the back, but these actions had no effect and he ordered the co-pilot to eject. Tait had heard the rear crew acknowledge his order to abandon the aircraft, but was unable to see if they had managed to get out because the blackout curtain was down behind him.

He had done everything he could. The Vulcan was now in a steep dive to port, and when he pulled the handle of his own ejection seat it was with the almost certain knowledge that it was too late to save himself; the Vulcan's nose-down attitude was such that he ought to have ejected straight into the ground.

It was only a miracle that saved him. As his seat's drogue parachute started to deploy, the seat and Tait passed between some high tension cables. These fouled the drogue, which caused a short, and the cables acted like arrester wires, braking the seat sharply and causing it to swing like a pendulum beneath them. It struck the ground fairly hard but in an upright position,

An Avro Vulcan B.2 bomber at low level over the English countryside. (MoD RAF)

enabling Tait to release himself and walk away, shaken but otherwise unhurt. Unfortunately, all four rear crew (which included a crew chief) were killed.

This crash resurrected the question of the lack of rear crew ejection seats, and caused a major outcry in the British Press. In the words of a *Daily Mirror* correspondent:

> *What precisely, do the men in the back of the V-bombers feel when they know that their pilot and co-pilot can eject themselves to safety, whereas they themselves need at least eight seconds to scramble out if the aircraft is about to crash? I expect no answers...*

The under-fuselage escape hatch was the only means of exit for the three Vulcan rear crew. (MoD RAF)

There were no real answers, but it should be remembered that out of seventy-one aircrew killed in sixteen V-bomber crashes between 1955 and 1968, of which seven involved Vulcans, twenty-one pilots and co-pilots also lost their lives, and some of them might have got out. So did they deliberately stay with the crashing aircraft, knowing that the rear crew had little or no chance of escaping? I put this question to Air Vice-Marshal Ron Dick, a former commanding officer of No 9 Squadron, who told me:

> Pilots would, naturally, make every effort to control the aircraft for as long as they could in an effort to get the rear crew out. You can imagine the scene: the pilot is trying to control the aircraft and at the same time peering over his shoulder to see what's happening in the back, knowing that it must be absolute bedlam in there. By the time he even thinks about ejecting, it is probably too late. I think maybe that's how the majority of V-bomber pilots were killed.

It might easily have been another tale of tragedy on 8 January 1971, when Flight Lieutenant Garth Alcock and his four-man crew faced an appalling emergency in a Vulcan B.2 (XM610) of No 44 Squadron. It happened during a low-level training sortie over Northumberland, when the Vulcan, based at RAF Waddington, in Lincolnshire, began to run into bad weather. Alcock decided to climb out of it, but as the engine power was increased there was a loud explosion and number one engine caught fire, followed quickly by number two engine. The crew took prompt action and reported that the fires appeared to have gone out, so Alcock held the Vulcan in its climb under the power to its to remaining engines and put out a distress call, turning south to head for RAF Leeming in North Yorkshire, a Master Diversion Airfield (MDA) where there were full crash and rescue facilities.

The labouring bomber reached 6000 feet, approaching the River Tyne. Things were looking more optimistic. If Alcock could maintain this altitude he should be able to reach Leeming, some 60 miles to the south, in just a few minutes.

Suddenly, the Vulcan's Air Electronics Operator, Flight Lieutenant Jim Power, raised the alarm. The flames had broken out again and part of the underside of the port wing was burning fiercely. Alcock, his hopes of making a safe landing dwindling with every second as the fire spread, flew on until the bomber was clear of cloud and over open country, when he ordered the three rear crew members – Jim Power and the two navigators, Flight Lieutenant James Vinales and Flying Officer Roger Baker – to bale out. All three made a safe descent and landed in fields near Rothbury. After landing they all operated their SARBE beacons, and within a few minutes a Whirlwind search and rescue helicopter from No 202 Squadron, RAF Boulmer, was homing onto them.

Now only Alcock and his co-pilot, Flying Officer Pete Hoskins, were left. Both had ejection seats, and knew that they could leave the crippled aircraft quickly if they had to. Neither knew how long the Vulcan would stay in the air, or whether it might explode at any moment; the port wing and rear fuselage were now well alight and the bomber was dragging a great banner of smoke in its wake. Yet, although the Vulcan was becoming increasingly difficult to control, Alcock knew that he had to hold on for as long as possible. The bomber was flying near the sprawling, densely populated Tyne conurbation, close to the city of Newcastle and its neighbouring towns of Gateshead and Sunderland, and what the outcome might be if it crashed there did not bear contemplation.

So Alcock and Hoskins remained in the shuddering cockpit for twelve more minutes, fighting together to hold the Vulcan on course, taking it safely over the populated areas and on past the historic city of Durham, turning out at last towards the coast. Pieces of molten, burning wreckage fell from the bomber as it staggered on, and at last Alcock felt his control slipping away. Reluctantly, for there were still some miles to run before he reached the sea, he ordered Hoskins to eject and prepared to follow suit. The Vulcan's cockpit roof flew away with a thud and Hoskins blasted out in his seat, leaving Alcock alone in what was now little more than eighty tons of blazing debris, dazed by the thunder of the airflow and the roar of fuel tanks that were now exploding one after the other.

And still he held on, for a few more desperate seconds, fighting to make sure that the aircraft would come down on open ground before he, too, pulled his seat handle and hurtled from the cockpit. Beneath him, as his parachute deployed, the flaming mass began its last plunge, roaring like a gigantic fireball over the village of Wingate to scatter its wreckage over several fields.

Those last few seconds had been vital. If Alcock had relinquished control just a fraction earlier, the bomber would have plunged into shops and houses. Alcock was subsequently awarded the Air Force Cross, and the other four crew members received the Queen's Commendation for Valuable Service in the Air.

Fate plays strange and often cruel tricks. On 14 October, 1975, Garth Alcock was the captain of one of the newer Vulcan B.2s, XM645, on detachment to Malta with a No 9 Squadron crew when the aircraft undershot the runway at RAF Luqa. The port undercarriage was pushed up into the wing, starting a fire as the aircraft bounced back into the air. Alcock managed to regain control and climbed to give the rear crew – who on this occasion were five in number – a chance to get out, but as he did so the fire caused an explosion and the aircraft started to break up. Alcock and his co-pilot ejected as the Vulcan disintegrated around them and escaped with their lives, but the other five were killed. A woman civilian was also killed by wreckage falling on the airfield, and two more civilians were injured when the main body of the debris fell on the adjacent village of Zabbar.

The Avro Vulcan

The first bomber in the world to employ the delta wing planform, the Avro Type 698 Vulcan prototype (VX770) flew for the first time on 30 August 1952, following extensive testing of its then radical configuration in the Avro 707 series of research deltas. The first prototype was fitted with four Rolls-Royce Avon turbojets and was later re-engined with Bristol Siddeley Sapphires and finally Rolls-Royce Conways, but the second prototype (VX777) employed Bristol Siddeley

Olympus 100s. This aircraft, which flew on 3 September 1953, featured a slightly lengthened fuselage and was later fitted with wings having redesigned leading edges with compound sweepback, flying in this configuration on 5 October 1955. It was later used to test the larger wing designed for the Vulcan B.Mk.2, being finally retired in 1960.

The first production Vulcan B.Mk.1 was delivered to No 230 Operational Conversion Unit in July 1956, and No 83 Squadron became the first unit to equip with the new bomber in July 1957. The second squadron to receive the aircraft, in October that year, was No 101, followed in May 1958 by No 617, the famous 'Dam Busters'. By this time production of the greatly improved Vulcan B.Mk.2 was well under way. The first production Vulcan B.2 flew on 30 August 1958, powered by Olympus 200 engines; the second production aircraft featured a bulged tailcone housing electronic countermeasures equipment, and this became standard on subsequent aircraft. Production of the B.Mk.1 was terminated with the forty-fifth aircraft, the remaining Vulcans on order being completed to B.Mk.2 standard with flight refuelling equipment, this model being designed to carry the American Skybolt air-launched IRBM. This was cancelled, but three Vulcan squadrons were armed with the Avro Blue Steel stand-off bomb. Meanwhile, the thirty-four Vulcan B.Mk.1s remaining in service were withdrawn for conversion to B.Mk.1A standard, which involved the fitting of new avionics, including full ECM. Conversion work was completed early in 1963. Units operating the B.1A were No 44 Squadron, which was formed at Waddington in Lincolnshire on 10 August 1960 by renumbering No 83; No 50, which re-formed in the following year; and No 101, as well as the Vulcan OCU. The Vulcan B.Mk.2 also received an avionics upgrade, including the fitting of terrain-following radar, and was then designated B.Mk.2A. Having relinquished the QRA (Quick Reaction Alert) role to the Polaris-armed nuclear submarines of the Royal Navy, the RAF's Vulcan force was assigned to NATO and CENTO in the free-fall bombing role. No 27 Squadron's B.2s also operated in the maritime radar reconnaissance (MRR) role for a time, their aircraft being redesignated Vulcan B.2 (MRR). In May 1982, Vulcans operating from Ascension Island in the Atlantic carried out attacks on the Falkland Islands in support of British operations to recapture these from Argentina. These operations, code-named 'Black Buck', involved both conventional bombing sorties and anti-radar missions by individual aircraft, each mission being supported by new fewer than eleven sorties by Victor K.2 tankers. Total Vulcan production was 136 aircraft, including the two prototypes and eighty-two B.2s. The last operational Vulcans were six aircraft of No 50 Squadron, converted to the flight refuelling role.

CHAPTER ELEVEN

FIGHT FOR SURVIVAL

S ometimes, a successful ejection has been only the preliminary to a far greater ordeal. Such was the case with Lieutenant David Steeves, a USAF pilot who, on the morning of 9 May 1957, took off in his T-33 jet from Hamilton Air Force base, California, on a routine training mission. He took the T-33 up to 38,000 feet and levelled off, cruising over the bleak, snow-patched wilderness of the High Sierra mountains. The minutes ticked by; everything was normal.

Then, without warning, Steeves' world exploded. He was slammed brutally forward in his straps and knocked into momentary oblivion. When he came to, the cockpit was full of smoke and the T-33 was spinning wildly. For a few

Lockheed T-33 jet trainers. David Steeves was flying one of these aircraft when his ordeal began. (Lockheed)

seconds he fought to regain control, then, realising that it was useless, he ejected.

The seat worked perfectly and Steeves was soon swinging under his parachute, conscious only of relief and cold and silence. Then his relief turned to sudden alarm as he felt instinctively that he was falling too fast. Looking up, he saw that two of the canopy's silken panels were torn. There was no time to worry about it now, and certainly nothing he could do about it. The snow-covered mountains seemed to be racing up to meet him. Seconds later, his feet smashed into a rocky ledge and he collapsed in a snowdrift.

Painfully, he dragged himself into a sitting position and explored his injuries. The impact had sprained both his ankles, which had already begun to swell. Apart from that, he appeared to have sustained only a few bruises.

Nevertheless, his position was serious enough. He was in the middle of a barren, icy waste, with nothing in his pockets but a revolver, a couple of half-used books of matches, some money, a pipe but no tobacco, and a photograph of his attractive wife, Rita, and their thirteen-month-old daughter Leisa. To make matters worse, he was wearing only a light summer uniform and was already blue with cold, shivering in the knife-edged wind that came howling down from the north-east.

With the wind came the first flakes of what promised to be a heavy snowfall. Laboriously, Steeves dragged himself into the shelter of some rocks and wrapped himself in the silk of his parachute. He was to remain huddled there for three days, completely without food, quenching his thirst with snow and ice.

By the fourth morning, he knew that there was no hope of rescue. There was only one thing for it: he had to start moving, or die. Gritting his teeth against the pain, he dragged himself to his feet and slowly, his head bowed against the biting wind, he began to stumble through the snow. When night fell, he scooped a hollow in the snow and lay down in it, sodden and weary, wrapped in some fragments of parachute silk he was using as a makeshift cloak. The whole exhausting pattern was repeated the next day... and the next... and the day after that.

Meanwhile, at her home in Trumbull, Connecticut, Steeves' wife was fighting a heartbreaking struggle against grief and anxiety. She had already received an official telegram, informing her that her husband was missing, and a few days later, a death certificate was issued. But Rita Steeves went on hoping, and waiting.

Towards the evening of his fifteenth day in the wilderness, Steves found himself in a canyon – and there, nestling between the sheer walls, was a log cabin. Inside, he found some cans on a shelf, containing ham and beans. There was a packet of dried soup, too, and some sugar. Tears streamed down the pilot's dirty, bearded cheeks as he broke open the cans with the aid of a rusty knife and ate his fill. Then, rolling himself in some sacking, he dropped into a deep, exhausted sleep.

The sun was high when he awoke the following day. Checking his small store of food, he discovered that in his ravenous hunger of the previous night he had eaten more than he had intended. The rest would soon be gone. During the next couple of days, however, Steeves occasionally caught a brief glimpse of deer in the canyon; they seemed to be using a well-trodden path, so the pilot devised a crude trap, lashing his cocked revolver to a sapling with one of his bootlaces and stretching a wire from the trigger to a nearby salt lick. He lined up the revolver carefully, banking on the chance that when one of the animals bent to lick the salt, it would touch the wire and spring the trap, sending a bullet through its head.

The trap worked early one morning, but Steeves failed to hear the shot because he was asleep. By the time he reached the carcass, most of it had been devoured by mountain lions. Nevertheless, he was able to salvage some of the meat, which he cut into strips and ate raw.

On his thirtieth day in the wilderness, Steeves decided that he was strong enough to make another attempt to reach civilisation, having obtained some extra rations in the way of trout, wild strawberries and an occasional snake. For two days, he toiled across the side of a mountain, searching for an easy way down, only to find his way barred by a raging torrent, fed by melting snow. He tried to get across, and almost drowned in the act. Utterly dispirited, he had no alternative but to return to his cabin. The daily struggle to find food was resumed, and added to this problem was another: the growing fear that he might lose his sanity.

On Sunday, 30 June 1957 – fifty-two days after he had parachuted from his crippled jet - Steeves left the canyon once more, this time heading in a different direction. In the evening of 1 July, after covering about twenty miles, he stumbled on two hunters, enjoying an evening meal by their campfire. The sight of Steeves staggering out of the dusk, his cheeks sunken and raked by thorns, his clothing in tatters, gave them a considerable shock; but they gave him some steak to eat and listened with growing incredulity as he choked out his story between mouthfuls. The next morning they took him to the nearest Air Force base, and to a world which had believed him dead for weeks.

Four years later, a USAF crew faced an ordeal of a different kind. It began when they were shot down by one of their own fighters. It began in April 1961, as a Boeing B-52 Stratofortress taxied slowly round the perimeter track of Biggs Air Force base near El Paso, Texas.

In the B-52's rear turret, isolated from the rest of the crew by 160 feet of slender fuselage, Sergeant Ray Singleton, the tail gunner, had little to do but glance at the parked B-52s of the 95th Bomb Wing as his own aircraft rolled past them. Over the intercom, he could hear the other seven crew members busy with their pre-flight checks. For the time being, Singleton could afford to relax. His turn to be vigilant would come later, 7 miles above the new Mexico desert, far beyond the layer of broken cloud that was spreading slowly across the sky.

A Boeing B-52H Stratofortress carrying four dummy Skybolt air-launched intermediate-range ballistic missiles. This weapon was later cancelled. (Boeing)

Not for the first time, Singleton felt intensely proud to be part of a first-rate fighting team. For Singleton and his crew, and the mighty bomber that carried them, were only small cogs in the giant machine of the United States Air Force's Strategic Air Command. Dispersed on bases throughout the United States, or on detachment overseas, were 549 more B-52s grouped in thirty-two bomb wings. Together – and not forgetting the medium jet bombers of the RAF's V-force – they formed the free world's nuclear deterrent. In time of war, every one of those Bomb Wings could have their aircraft off the ground in minutes, fanning out as they climbed to minimise the effects of nuclear blast in case their bases were about to come under sudden attack. Then they would head towards their targets somewhere deep in the heart of the Soviet Union. One-third of the B-52 force was always airborne, ready to retaliate instantly if the West came under surprise attack.

Despite their doomsday role the men of Strategic Air Command were always conscious that their task was to prevent war, not to start it. Inside every SAC crew-room, a large sign proclaimed: 'Peace is Our Profession'. And that just about summed it up. If SAC and the other nuclear strike forces of the free world ever ceased to deter a potential aggressor, then the world would be free no longer.

The B-52, SAC's formidable spearhead, was the most remarkable strategic bomber ever built. It traced its ancestry back to the Second World War and the piston-engined Boeing B-29 Superfortress, the aircraft that enabled the Americans to conduct a shattering long-range bombing offensive against Japan in 1945, culminating in the dropping of atomic bombs on Hiroshima and Nagasaki.

In September 1945, only days after the end of the war, the Boeing Aircraft Company began design work on a new jet bomber to replace the B-29. The new aircraft, which emerged as the B-47 Stratojet, was a radical departure from conventional design, featuring a thin, flexible swept wing – based on wartime German research data – on which six turbojets were mounted in underwing pods. A thousand Stratojets had been delivered to the USAF by the end of 1954, and the bulk of SAC's bomber wings were equipped with the type until 1955, when the B-52 began to enter service.

The B-52, which first flew in 1951, was much larger and heavier than the B-47. The first production version, the B-52B – the model that equipped the 95th Bomb Wing – weighed close on 180 tons fully laden. Its wings spanned 185 feet, and under the power of its eight Pratt & Whitney J57 turbojets it could climb to 55,000 feet, reach a speed of over 630 mph and fly 9000 miles without refuelling.

The B-52 was thus the 'Big Stick' of America's nuclear deterrent forces, filling the dangerous gap that existed until nuclear-powered ballistic missile submarines and intercontinental ballistic missiles were available in sufficient numbers. And during the dangerous years of the late 1950s and early 1960s SAC's efficiency depended on one factor above all others: constant, rigorous training, so that each crew, each squadron, each wing became welded together like a single entity, supremely confident of its ability to carry out his mission.

That was why, on this morning of 7 April 1961, Singleton's B-52 was taxiing out towards the end of the runway at Biggs Air Force Base. The crew had gone through their flight plan during a lengthy briefing session the day before; it involved flying a series of dog-leg courses across half the North American continent, locating and bombing a series of selected targets from high alitude with the aid of radar. The bombing, of course, would be simulated, for on training flights the B-52's huge bomb bay was empty. There was a strong element of competition involved, too, for in the course of an air exercise lasting several days the SAC crew that emerged with the best navigation and simulated bombing results would receive a coveted trophy for their Wing.

There would also be opposition. Somewhere over New Mexico, the B-52 was scheduled to be intercepted by 'enemy' fighters. They would, in fact, be aircraft of the Air National Guard (ANG), the territorial force raised by each US state. Although composed mainly of part-time reserve personnel, the ANG flew modern aircraft and formed an important operational element of the USAF. In times of crisis, such as the Korean War, ANG units were brought into active service, flying combat missions alongside regular USAF squadrons. Like SAC, their efficiency and operational readiness depended on the highest possible level of training.

The B-52 turned on to the main runway, and Ray Singleton, strapped in his turret at the base of the bomber's forty-foot-high tail fin, felt the surge of acceleration as the engines opened up to full power. The runway blurred underneath him, then fell away as the aircraft commander, Captain Don Blodgett, lifted the big bird cleanly away. Streams of black smoke from the B-52's engines swept past Singleton's turret as the bomber climbed steeply towards the overcast.

The intercom chatter continued as the crew went on with their flight checks. Every member of the crew, officers and enlisted men alike, knew one another as intimately as if they had been brought up together. In the air, rank was of secondary importance. The main thing was teamwork, with each man knowing precisely what he had to do. Mentally, Singleton ticked off the names of the crew. Seated next to Blodgett, in the B-52's roomy cockpit, was the co-pilot, Captain Ray Obel. Behind them were the two navigators, Captain Peter Gineris and Captain Steve Carter. The latter was lucky to be alive; only the year before, he had been the sole survivor of a B-47 which had plunged into the sea off the Azores. Then came the air warfare officer, Captain George Jackson, and the air electronics officer, Second Lieutenant Glen Bair. Last, but far from least, was Sergeant Manual Mieras, the crew chief, whose task was to check out the B-52's systems, supervise ground handling and ensure that the whole machine was completely serviceable and airworthy before each flight. He knew the giant bomber inside out.

The B-52 broke through the overcast and climbed to its operational height of 36,000 feet, the brilliant sunshine glinting on its light grey upper surfaces. The bomber's underside was painted white to give protection from the flash of her thermonuclear weapons, if ever she had to fly the doomsday mission. On her nose, just under the cockpit, was painted the name *Ciudad Juarez*, after El Paso's sister town just across the border in Mexico.

Seven miles up in the sky the bomber plunged on through the dazzling, rarified air at a speed of nearly 10 miles a minute, dragging a broad white vapour trail in her wake. Two hours later she reached the first turning point of the exercise, right on time. The navigators were spot on, as usual, and their efforts drew a brief word of praise from Blodgett. With his thumb and index finger, he turned the knob of the autopilot control slightly and brought the massive aircraft round in a gentle turn, heading for the next target, and called up Ray Singleton as he did so.

Tail gunner, this is AC.
AC, this is tail gunner, go ahead.
Ray, those National Guard planes are scheduled to make some passes at us pretty soon. Keep your eyes open for them.
Roger, sir.

Singleton became alert at once, peering beyond the barrels of his twin 20-

millimetre cannon, searching the burning expanse of sky for a glimpse of tell-tale contrails. In time of war, the keenness of his eyes might mean the difference between life and death for the eight men on board the B-52. Admittedly, his position was equipped with airborne warning radar, but his eyes were the decisive factor in determining whether an approaching aircraft was hostile or friendly.

Still many miles away, high over the New Mexico desert, a pair of F-100 Super Sabres of the Air National Guard's 188th Fighter Interceptor Squadron from Kirtland Air Force Base, near Albuquerque, swung around in a wide circle, cruising almost lazily to conserve fuel while they awaited instructions from 'Blush First', the local Ground Controlled Intercept station. The pilot of the leading aircraft was First Lieutenant James 'Sock' Van Sycoc, a sturdy, dark-haired regular USAF officer with ten years' service and 1900 hours' flying time behind him, 1000 of them on Super Sabres. His wingman was a National Guard pilot, Captain Dale Dodd.

The North American F-100 was a potent interceptor. Born during the years of the Korean War, it incorporated many of the lessons learned by the pilots of its predecessor, the famous F-86 Sabre, in combat against Russian MiG-15 jets. The first operational aircraft in the world capable of exceeding the speed of sound in level flight, the F-100 later established several world air speed records. It carried a powerful armament of four 20-mm cannon in the nose, and two Sidewinder heat-seeking air-to-air missiles on pylons under its wings.

The F-100s flown by Van Sycoc and Dodd were both armed and ready for combat. Although this was a training flight, the pilots might have to intercept an unidentified aircraft; and if that aircraft turned out to be hostile, they would have to shoot it down.

Crackling over Van Sycoc's headphones, the voice of the GCI controller came up with the information on the altitude of the approaching B-52, and the course the fighters would have to steer to intercept it. Both pilots now carried out a vital part of the procedure: the armament safety check. Their gloved hands moved over the console positioned at the side of the instrument-packed cockpit, checking a battery of switches and circuit breakers. Everything was on 'safe', which meant that neither the cannon nor the Sidewinders could be fired. Van Sycoc and Dodd both confirmed this to the GCI controller.

With their weapons now inert the F-100s streaked towards their target. A few moments later, a shimmering blip appeared on Van Sycoc's radar screen: the B-52. Van Sycoc called 'Tally Ho' over the radio and the two F-100s formed up for a simulated missile attack, curving in sharply and reducing speed once more, their wings glittering in the harsh sunlight. In the B-52's cockpit, Captain Ray Obel caught sight of them as they flashed past, rolling into a turn for a second attack. From his position in the tail turret, Ray Singleton, who had alerted the crew to the fighters' approach, watched fascinated as the Super Sabres flashed past again and again, making simulated cannon-firing passes as he tracked them with his own guns.

Van Sycoc glanced at his fuel gauges, and called up Dodd.

Okay, he said. *One more run, and then we'll go home.*

The fighters closed in for another simulated missile pass, lining up astern of the B-52 and streaking over the swirling contrail. In a real attack, the missiles would home in on the hot exhaust gases pouring from the bomber's engines. Van Sycoc's F-100, in the lead, rapidly overhauled the Stratofortress. The pilot watched the bomber's big tail and long, flexing wings loom bigger and bigger in his sights.

Suddenly, his aircraft seemed to jerk slightly. Something leaped ahead of it and streaked towards the bomber – a glowing thing with a fiery trail, dragging a long smoke trail.

Van Sycoc's heart leaped into his mouth. Frantically, he pressed the transmit button and yelled a warning over his radio.

Look out – one of my missiles has fired!

It was too late. With unerring accuracy, the Sidewinder sped straight towards the target, the hot, pulsing gases churning out behind a pair of the B-52's engines, slung in their pod under the huge port wing. There was a vivid orange flash, a gush of black smoke, and the stricken B-52 reared up and rolled sharply to the left, spewing chunks of burning metal.

In the Stratofortress's cockpit, Blodgett and Obel heard Van Sycoc's frantic warning shout. A few seconds later, they were crushed into their seats as the great bomber swung crazily over on its wing-tip. For a few moments Blodgett wrestled with the controls, helplessly, as the B-52 twisted out of the sky. Then, quickly ordering the rest of the crew to bale out. He pulled the handles of his ejection seat and felt himself blasted out into space.

In the tail turret, Ray Singleton had been bewildered by the sheer speed of the disaster. He had caught a brief glimpse of the Sidewinder's black smoke trail, and had been stunned by the numbing shock of the impact. Dimly, he heard Blodgett order the crew to abandon the aircraft. He jettisoned his turret, unfastened his seat harness and tumbled out into the slipstream – straight into the roaring, agonising river of flame that poured back in the bomber's wake. He hung there for what seemed an eternity, suspended in the searing inferno, and then mercifully he was falling away, dropping through the clean, freezing sky.

Up above, the two fighter pilots watched in horror as the shattered remains of the B-52 plunged into the cloud layer below. They could see no sign of any parachutes. Transmitting emergency signals, Van Sycoc and Dodd let down cautiously into the swirling vapour. They had to be careful, for somewhere in all this murk was the 11,400-foot peak of Mount Taylor. It was no use; they could see nothing. The clouds extended right down to 6000 feet, almost to the level of the high plateau of the New Mexican desert. Cramming on the power, the pilots lifted their Super Sabres out of the cotton wool and set course for Kirtland Air Force Base.

Kirtland, alerted by Van Sycoc's distress call, was a hive of activity. One of the biggest USAF bases, it handled a large amount of air traffic, both military and civilian. Consequently, its search and rescue facilities were among the best to be found anywhere. As the two F-100s landed, four rescue helicopters were preparing to take off, the clatter of their rotors adding to the din made by three T-33 jet trainers which were just climbing away from the runway to take part in the search.

The wreckage of the B-52 lay 9000 feet high on the slopes of Mount Taylor. Because the fighter pilots had reported seeing no parachutes, the rescuers who toiled towards it did not entertain much hope that there would be any survivors. To make matters worse, a cold front was moving in and visibility was getting steadily worse as the rescue aircraft roared back and forth over the craggy rocks.

Then, within five hours of the tragedy, came the electrifying news that a survivor had been sighted. It was Blodgett. His pelvis was fractured and he was unable to move. He was spotted by the pilot of a T-33 jet, who guided a Kaman H-43 rescue helicopter to his position. A few minutes later, the same jet pilot sighted a second survivor: Ray Singleton. The tail gunner was badly burned about the face as a result of his fall through the flames that streamed from the shattered bomber.

The helicopter was just climbing away, with Blodgett and Singleton safely on board, when the latter shouted that he had seen another parachute. The Kaman descended again, and this time found Captain George Jackson, the air warfare officer. His back was broken. Gently, the rescuers lifted him into the helicopter, which took off and headed back to Kirtland at top speed. It was almost incredible that the three injured men had fallen so close together, and the fact probably saved their lives. Not long after they were picked up the temperature dropped almost to zero and a raging storm blasted over the crash area, accompanied by freezing 70mph winds. Blodgett and Jackson, incapacitated by their injuries, would almost certainly have succumbed to exposure.

All that night and the next day the storm howled, bringing the rescue operation to a standstill. The helicopter pilots, with great courage and disregard for their own safety, went on flying as long as they could, but before long even taking off became impossible. Only one ground party managed to battle its way up Mount Taylor to reach the place where the wreckage of the B-52 lay, strewn in a smoking, blackened mass around a huge crater. Beneath that heap of charred and twisted metal lay the bodies of the air electronics officer, Glen Bair, and the two navigators, Pete Gineris and Steve Carter. Death, which Carter had cheated by a hair's breadth in the Atlantic only months earlier, had claimed him in the end.

On 9 April, after the storm had blown itself out, the flash of a hand mirror brought a rescuer to yet another of the survivors. It was the crew chief, Sergeant Manuel Mieras. When the aircraft broke up, he had found himself suddenly hanging in space under his parachute. He had no idea how he had got clear of the aircraft. He broke a leg on landing, but fashioned a makeshift crutch from a tree branch and managed to hobble as far as a shepherd's hut, where he had sheltered from the elements until the rescue aircraft flew overhead.

It was a flashing mirror, too, that drew the searchers to the co-pilot, Captain Ray Obel. He was suffering from shock; his parachute, which should not have opened until he reached 10,000 feet, had actually deployed 20,000 higher up with a terrific jolt, and Obel had suffered badly from the cold during his long descent. Adding to his ordeal, he had landed right in the middle of a cactus patch. After he had picked dozens of painful spines from his face and hands, he spent the next day and night wrapped in his parachute, with his inflatable life-raft pulled over him for shelter.

Three men had died; five others were saved. And now came the searching inquiry: why had Van Sycoc's missile fired?

It was quickly established that the pilot had been in no way to blame, and that all the proper safeguards against an accidental launch had been meticulously carried out. One thing above all puzzled the investigators; both Sidewinders had been carried under one wing of Van Sycoc's F-100, the pylon under the other wing having been occupied by a fuel tank, and for aerodynamic reasons the outer missile could only be fired after the inner one. Yet it was the outer Sidewinder that had destroyed the B-52 – a technical impossibility.

Only when the missile firing circuits were stripped down did the amazing answer come to light. A tiny blot of moisture in the system had been to blame. In a million-to-one chance, an impulse from the F-100's electrical system had passed through the blot into the missile firing circuit. The Sidewinder had launched itself, and the bomber had gone down in flames.

The Boeing B-52 Stratofortress

During the dangerous years of the 1960s, the mighty Boeing B-52 was the symbol of America's awesome striking power. Few could have imagined that it would still be in first-line service, half a century after the prototype first flew. It remained the core of the West's airborne strategic bomber forces ever since it entered service with the USAF Strategic Air Command in 1955, its operational career spanning almost all the Cold War era. In addition, the B-52 has experienced the full range of technical and operational changes that have proven necessary to enable the strategic bomber to survive in an intensely hostile environment, particularly one dominated by sophisticated surface-to-air missiles.

The B-52 was the product of a USAAF requirement, issued in April 1946, for a new jet heavy bomber to replace the Convair B-36 in Strategic Air Command. Two prototypes were ordered in September 1949, the YB-52 flying for the first time on 15 April 1952 powered by eight Pratt & Whitney J57-P-3 turbojets. On 2 October 1952 the XB-52 also made its first flight, both aircraft having the same powerplant. The two B-52 prototypes were followed by three B-52As, the first of which flew on 5 August 1954. These aircraft featured a number of modifications and were used for extensive trials, which were still in progress when the first production B-52B was accepted by SAC's 93rd Bomb Wing at Castle AFB, California. Fifty examples were produced for SAC (including ten of the thirteen B-52As originally ordered, which were converted to B-52B standard) and it was followed on the production line by the B-52C, thirty-five of which were built. The focus of B-52 production then shifted to Wichita with the appearance of the B-52D, the first of which flew on 14 May 1956; 170 were eventually built. Following the B-52E (100 built) and the B-52F (eighty-nine) came the major production variant, the B-52G. The B-52G was the first aircraft to be armed with a long-range stand-off air-to-surface missile, the North American GAM-77 Hound Dog, a system designed to enhance the bomber's chances of survival. The missile was designed to carry a one-megaton warhead over a range of between 500 and 700nm (926 and 1,297km) depending on the mission profile, and could operate between tree-top level and 55,000ft (16,775m) at speeds of up to 2.1M. The weapon was fitted with a North American Autonetics Division inertial system, which was linked to the aircraft's navigation systems and continually updated by a Kollsman astro-tracker in the launch pylon. All B-52Gs and, later, B-52Hs armed with the Hound Dog carried one pylon-mounted round under each wing. The Hound Dogs' turbojets were lit up during take-off, effectively making the B-52 a ten-engined aircraft, and were subsequently shut down, the missile's tanks being topped up from the parent aircraft. After launch, the missile could follow a high or low flight profile, with dog legs and diversions as necessary. Later, anti-radar and terrain contour matching (TERCOM) modifications were introduced. At the missile's peak in 1962 there were 592 Hound Dogs on SAC's inventory, and it is a measure of the system's effectiveness that it remained in operational service until 1976. B-52G production totalled 193 examples, 173 of these being converted in the 1980s to carry twelve Boeing AGM-86B Air Launched Cruise Missiles. The last version was the B-52H, which had been intended to carry the cancelled Skybolt air-launched IRBM but was modified to carry four Hound Dogs instead. The B-52 was also armed with the Short-Range Attack Missile (SRAM). The first being delivered to the 42nd Bomb Wing at Loring AFB, Maine, on 4 March 1972. The B-52 was capable of carrying twenty SRAMs, twelve in three-round underwing clusters and eight in the aft bomb bay, together with up to four Mk 28 thermonuclear weapons.

The B-52 was the mainstay of the West's airborne nuclear deterrent forces for three decades, but it was in a conventional role that it went to war, first over Vietnam, then in the Gulf War of 1991, and more latterly in support of NATO operations in the former Yugoslavia. In all, 729 B-52 sorties were flown during the Linebacker II bombing offensive in Vietnam, and more than 15,000 tons of bombs dropped out of a total of 20,370 tons. Fifteen B-52swere lost to the SAM defences, and nine damaged. Thirty-four targets had been hit, and some 1,500 civilians killed. Of the ninety-two crew members aboard the shot-down bombers, twenty-six were recovered by rescue teams, twenty-nine were listed as missing, and thirty-three baled out over North Vietnam to be taken prisoner and later repatriated.The later variants of the B-52 were extensively rebuilt and upgraded during the bomber's long career, which has encompassed operations in Afghanistan and Iraq.

CHAPTER TWELVE

DANGEROUS DESCENTS

In the 1950s, with aircraft speeds and altitudes being pushed continually higher, the problems of crew escape increased in direct proportion. No pilots were more aware of these problems than the men who flew high-speed, high-altitude rocket research aircraft on both sides of the Iron Curtain. Death was never far from any of them, whenever they flew, for no matter how perfectly everything checked out, you always had to expect the unexpected where rockets were concerned.

One of the men who knew that better than most was Colonel Charles E. 'Chuck' Yeager, the first man to fly faster than sound in 1947, in the cockpit of a Bell XS-1 rocket aircraft. Sixteen years later Yeager, still a test pilot, was responsible for testing the Lockheed NF-104A, a modified version of the basic F-104 Starfighter with a rocket motor mounted under the fuselage. Three such aircraft belonged to the Aerospace Research Pilot School, commanded by Yeager, at Edwards Air Force Base, California, and were used for training future astronauts in ballistic flight techniques.

The idea was that the NF-104A would accelerate in level flight until Mach 2.15 was reached under the power of its jet and rocket motors, then pull up into a zoom climb. The jet engine would be cut off as the aircraft passed through 80,000 feet and the NF-104A would be boosted up to heights of over 100,000 feet by the rocket. As it coasted 'over the top', the trainee-astronaut pilot would experience a state of weightlessness, during which he had to carry out a variety of tasks.

When Yeager was testing one of these aircraft in December 1963, things went badly wrong; at 104,000 feet (nearly 21 miles up) the rocket motor flamed out. Without engine power, the main engine having been shut down, there was no hydraulic control for the flight controls, and because of the height at which the rocket motor had flamed out, manual control was impossible. As the aircraft fell into a flat spin, Yeager deployed the spin recovery parachute in an attempt to get the aircraft into an attitude where he might be able to relight the turbojet, but without success. The aircraft made fourteen complete flat spins on its way to the desert floor, and Yeager stayed with it for thirteen of them, desperately trying to save the NF-104A. He ejected at 8,500 feet in his full pressure suit, his rocket-propelled seat carrying him clear of the tumbling aircraft.

Yeager successfully separated from the seat, but after separation the pilot was struck by the seat, which had a lower coefficient of drag than he did and therefore fell faster than him. The rocket motor struck his helmet, which was being fed oxygen from the emergency survival kit, and shattered the visor. Some residual solid fuel propellant still burned in the seat rocket motors, and

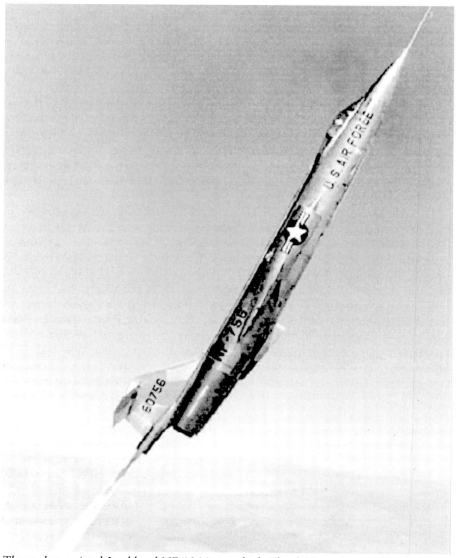

The rocket-assisted Lockheed NF-104A, in which Chuck Yeager came close to losing his life. (USAF Museum)

this set fire to the pilot's pressure suit and the oxygen flowing through his helmet. With his face in the middle of an inferno, choking on the smoke and stench of his own burning flesh, Yeager managed to push up what was left of his visor and shut off the flow of oxygen, extinguishing the flames. The pilot landed safely, although his face and hands were badly charred. He was in hospital for a month.

Much thought was also being given in the late 1950s and early 1960s to the problems of ejecting from a spacecraft within the earth's atmosphere. Early Russian spacecraft were equipped with ejection seats, which were used by the crew to bale out of a space capsule during the final stage of descent through the earth's atmosphere after a mission, but American astronauts enjoyed no such luxury, relying on a spacecraft's parachutes to deploy and bring it – and them – down to a 'soft' landing.

One of the main problems encountered in ejecting from a spacecraft or aircraft at extreme altitudes was stabilisation. With practically no air resistance, a crew member might encounter uncontrolled tumbling and spinning of up to 200 revolutions per minute, producing a life-threatening situation. To investigate the physical problem the USAF and NASA set up Project Excelsior, whose director was a remarkable man named Joseph Kittinger.

Joseph Kittinger was born on 27 July 1928, and grew up near Orlando, Florida. He became fascinated with aircraft at a very early age when he saw a Ford Trimotor at a nearby airport. As a youth, he persuaded local pilots to give him free rides, and he soloed in a Piper Cub by the time he was 17. Kittinger attended the University of Florida for two years, then left to join the U.S. Air Force in 1949 as an aviation cadet and earn his wings. He served as a NATO test pilot in Germany until 1953, when he was assigned to the Air Force Missile Development Center at Holloman Air Force Base in New Mexico. At Holloman, Captain Kittinger flew experimental jet fighters and participated in aerospace medical research. In 1955, he flew the T-33 observation aircraft that monitored the 'rocket-sled' experiments carried out by aircraft medicine pioneer Colonel John Paul Stapp, in which Stapp took his sled to speeds of over 630 mph to test how rapid acceleration and deceleration physically affected the human body.

Stapp recruited Kittinger for Project Man High, a project begun in 1955 using balloons capable of high-altitude flight and a pressurised gondola (the basket or capsule suspended from the balloon) to study cosmic rays and to determine if humans were physically and psychologically capable of extended travel at space-like altitudes (above ninety-nine per cent of the Earth's atmosphere). The Air Force had determined that a high-altitude balloon flight was the best way to conduct these studies since aircraft could only remain at these altitudes for periods of time that were too short to provide useful data. Using a two-million-cubic-foot, 172.6-foot diameter balloon and a cramped aluminium alloy capsule manufactured by Winzen Research of Minneapolis, Kittinger made the first Man High ascent on 2 June, 1957, remaining aloft for almost seven hours and climbing to 96,000 feet. The lessons learned from his flight and two other Man High flights later in 1957 and in 1958 by Major David Simons and Lieutenant Clifton McClure, that went even higher and set new records, proved invaluable later in NASA's Project Mercury.

In 1958, Kittinger moved to the Escape Section of the Aeromedical Laboratory at Wright Air Development Center's Aero Medical Laboratory. There, he joined Project Excelsior, which investigated the use of a parachute

Joseph Kittinger, Jr. (USAF Museum)

for escape from a space capsule or high-altitude aircraft. At the time no one knew whether humans could survive a jump from the edge of space.

On 16 November, 1959, Kittinger ascended in Excelsior I to 76,000 feet and returned to Earth by jumping, free falling, and parachuting to the desert floor in New Mexico. The jump almost cost him his life. His small parachute, which served to stabilise him and prevent him from going into a fatal flat spin, opened after only two seconds of free fall instead of sixteen, catching Kittinger around the neck and causing him to spiral uncontrollably. Soon he lost consciousness, as he tumbled toward the ground at 120 revolutions per minute. Only his emergency parachute, which opened automatically at 10,000 feet, saved his life.

In spite of this close call, Kittinger persevered with the project and ascended in Excelsior II, on 11 December, 1959. This balloon climbed to 74,700 feet before Kittinger jumped from the gondola, setting a free-fall record of 55,000 feet before pulling his parachute ripcord.

In the next year, Kittinger established two more records. On 16 August, 1960, Kittinger surpassed the altitude record set by Major David Simons, who had climbed to 101,516 feet in 1957 in his Man-High II balloon. Kittinger ascended to 102,800 feet in Excelsior III, an open gondola adorned with a paper licence plate that his five-year-old son had cut out of a cereal box. Protected against the subzero temperatures by layers of clothes and a pressure suit – he experienced air temperatures as low as minus 94 degrees Fahrenheit (minus 70 degrees Celsius) – and loaded down with gear that almost doubled his weight, he climbed to his maximum altitude in one hour and thirty-one minutes, even though at 43,000 feet he began experiencing severe pain in his right hand caused by a failure in his pressure glove that could have led to the mission being aborted. He remained at peak altitude for about twelve minutes; then he stepped out of his gondola into the darkness of space. After falling for thirteen seconds, his six-foot diameter parachute opened and stabilised his fall, preventing the flat spin that could have killed him. Only four minutes and thirty-six seconds more were needed to bring him down to about 17,500 feet, where his regular 28-foot parachute opened. His descent set another record for the longest parachute freefall.

During his descent, he reached speeds up to 614 miles per hour, approaching the speed of sound without the protection of an aircraft or space

Joseph Kittinger makes his exit from the Excelsior III balloon at 102,800 feet on 16 August 1960. (USAF)

vehicle. He said later that he had absolutely no sense of the speed. His flight and parachute jump demonstrated that, properly protected, it was possible to put a person into near-space and that airmen could exit their aircraft at extremely high altitudes and free-fall back into the Earth's atmosphere without dangerous consequences.

After Excelsior, Kittinger moved on to Project Stargazer, which began in January 1959. This balloon astronomy experiment studied high-altitude astronomical phenomena from above ninety-five per cent of the Earth's atmosphere. This vantage point allowed undistorted visual and photographic observations of the stars and planets. On 13-14 December, 1962, Kittinger, along with astronomer William C. White, rose to an altitude of 82,200 feet and hovered over Holloman Air Force Base in the Stargazer gondola. The two checked variations in the brightness of star images caused by the atmosphere and made observations by telescope. The flight also provided useful information about the development of pressure and associated life support systems during an extended period on the edge of space.

Kittinger later volunteered for three combat tours in Vietnam, flying 483 missions. On 11 May 1972, he was shot down and spent eleven months in captivity as a prisoner of war.

After his retirement, he continued working in aeronautics. He won the Gordon Bennett Gas Balloon Race four times during the 1980s and retained the trophy with three consecutive victories. In November 1983, Kittinger established a new world record by flying a 35,300 cubic-foot helium balloon from Las Vegas, Nevada, to Franklinville, New York, covering 2,001 miles in seventy-two hours. He expended all available ballast during this trip and landed in only his underwear. In September 1984, Kittinger set another record by flying solo across the Atlantic Ocean. He flew the 105,944-cubic-foot helium-filled *Rosie O'Grady* from Presque Island, Maine to the Italian Riviera near Savona, Italy. His trip covered 3,535 miles in eighty-six hours.

It is not generally known that Kittinger had a Russian counterpart. He was Colonel Eugenii Nikolaevich Andreev, who tested more than 200 types of parachute, emergency extraction systems and space suits between 1947 and 1986 on behalf of the Soviet Air Force's Scientific Research Institute. Andreev jumped from more than fifty different types of aircraft and held eight records, including being the first person to jump from an altitude of 25.5 kilometres (15.8 miles). Andreev was made a Hero of the Soviet Union.

Eighteen months before Kittinger made his first high-altitude jump from Excelsior I, two RAF aircrew broke the record for the highest emergency ejection using a Martin-Baker seat. They were Flight Lieutenant Peter de Salis and Flying Officer Peter Lowe, the crew of an English Electric Canberra jet bomber of No 76 Squadron. Canberras were involved almost from the outset in Britain's nuclear weapons programme, carrying out radiation sampling and other associated duties. In 1957, after various atomic devices had been tested at Monte Bello and in Australia, the stage was set for Britain to explode her first thermonuclear device at Christmas Island in the Pacific (or, more correctly, at Malden Island, some 400 miles to the south of the main Christmas Island base).

Because of the expected magnitude of the H-bomb explosion, it was anticipated that the Canberras would have problems in reaching the required operational altitude of 56,000 feet or more during their sampling missions, and so plans were made to fit a Napier Double Scorpion rocket motor in two Canberra B.Mk.6s of No 76 Squadron. The liquid-fuelled Scorpion, selected originally to give extra boost to the English Electric Lightning interceptor (but never used, because the Lightning could easily reach 70,000 feet or more under the power of its Rolls-Royce Avon RA.24 turbojets) was test-flown in May 1956 in Canberra B.2 WK163, and in this Double Scorpion form it helped power this aircraft to a new world altitude record of 70,310 feet on 28 August 1957.

The two Canberras of No 76 Squadron fitted with the Double Scorpion installation were WT206 and WT207. A third aircraft, WT208, was also experimentally fitted with a de Havilland Spectre rocket motor, but was not assigned to the H-bomb tests.

The two rocket-assisted Canberras carried out numerous radiation sampling missions from Christmas Island during 1957, the first British

Record-breaking Canberra WK163 pictured during trials with the Napier Scorpion rocket motor. (Author's collection)

hydrogen bomb being air-dropped from a Vickers Valiant of No 49 Squadron on 15 May that year. The tests culminated in an air-drop of the weapon in its operational configuration on 8 November. On returning to the United Kingdom, WT207 was loaned to Napiers for further rocket motor tests, and it was while carrying out one of these, on 9 April 1958, that the rocket motor – which was recessed into the bomb bay – exploded.

At first, Flight Lieutenant de Salis and Flying Officer Lowe did not know what had happened, but then the Canberra began to disintegrate around them and they ejected into an outside air temperature of minus 57 degrees Centigrade at 56,000 feet. Both men had traumatic descents; Lowe free-fell to

10,000 feet, where his parachute opened automatically, and landed in a farmer's field, suffering a back injury. De Salis had a worse time of it, his seat having malfunctioned. Spinning at four revolutions per second, it fell for 30,000 feet before it separated from the pilot and his parachute deployed. De Salis, suffering from frostbite and almost totally incapacitated after his long, spinning drop, somehow managed to untangle the shroud lines, which had become twisted, and made a safe landing. The remains of the aircraft fell at Monyash, near Bakewell, Derbyshire.

A few days after this episode, on 30 April 1958, two Experimental Officers with the Aerodynamics Flight Section, RAE Bedford, had a lucky escape when they ascended in a tethered balloon over Larkhill artillery range, Wiltshire, to drop a scale model of the Bristol Type 188 research aircraft. At 5500 feet, the balloon cable was accidentally released from the winch. The balloon continued to ascend, and at 10,000 feet, still going up, the two occupants decided it was time to bale out. This they did successfully, then saw to their dismay that they were descending into Larkhill West Down artillery shelling area, and that a shoot was in progress. Fortunately, somebody saw them coming down and called a ceasefire.

* * * *

It is an old saying among pilots that no one would persuade them to jump out of a perfectly serviceable aircraft; but paratroopers do just that, and sometimes they encounter trouble.

The possibility that a parachute might open prematurely and become entangled with the aircraft is a nightmare scenario that crosses the minds of most parachutists, and in the case of a French paratrooper, Private Daniel Minne, it became a reality. In 1959, Minne, a 20-year-old soldier with the 40th French North African Paratroop Squadron, was making a practice jump from a Nord Noratlas transport 13,000 feet over the Sahara Desert, 100 miles south-west of Algiers, when things went wrong.

> *I felt a jerk at the parachute and then a violent tug, as if someone were trying to tear my shoulders from my body. Then I knew that something had gone wrong. My eyes were still closed, but I wasn't dropping: the cold sensation of vertigo, as you fall through space or dangle at the end of parachute cords, was strangely absent. The initial tug at my shoulders became an excruciating agony, and, as I opened my eyes, the full blast of the slipstream caught me smack in the face. Particles of dust in the air, driven back by the propellers, punctured my face and tore at my eyes as I was spun out behind the plane. I waited to fall clear and drift down to the desert below, but as I forced my eyes open again, I saw to my complete horror that I was trailing along behind the plane.*

Minne was floating in mid-air about twenty feet behind the Noratlas, his parachute canopy entangled with the tail. He began to spin, slowly at first, then faster, so that the parachute harness bit painfully into his chest. Grasping

A Nord Noratlas transport aircraft. (Author's collection)

the nylon shroud lines, he tried to drag himself hand over hand towards the aircraft, but it was useless. His only comfort was that he had an emergency 'chute clipped to his chest. As a last resort, he could cut himself free and use that.

Then, sickeningly, the Noratlas began to climb and dive steeply as the pilot, Captain Dupuis, tried every trick in the book to shake Minne free. The manoeuvres served only to exacerbate the paratrooper's problems; he could not breath and felt that he was being strangled by the collar of his flight jacket. Sand, drifting up from the desert, filled his nose, ears and eyes, and the nylon cords twisted around his waist felt as though they were about to cut him in two.

> *Through a bloody haze now filming my eyes, I saw the men in the box car struggling to manoeuvre something long through the doorway towards me. It was a hooked fork at the end of which appeared to be a stick. I guessed that they were trying to hook me into the plane. The home-made grapnel came within inches of the twisted nylon cord but just wasn't long enough to hook over it.*

Minne reasoned that it was time to cut himself loose, but when he tried to grasp his bayonet he found it impossible. The nylon cords had torn his hands to such an extent that he could not close them enough to make a fist.

Further attempts to rescue Minne, including one with a helicopter trailing a rope ladder, also failed. Minne saw that the Noratlas was circling its base at Boufarik at about 2000 feet, the pilot clearly intent on making a landing. Minne resigned himself to being dragged along the runway at high speed as the aircraft touched down.

Then, as the Noratlas made its final approach, he realised that the little emergency parachute might yet save him. He managed to hook his fingers

French paratroops carrying out a massed drop.
(Armand Agababian)

around the D-ring, and just before his body touched the ground he pulled it.

I saw its white canopy billow open above me and jerk me upwards, filled by the slipstream. Now the plane was speeding along the landing strip and I was being hauled along behind her, at 90 mph, with the little parachute, not much bigger than a beach umbrella, keeping me just clear of the concrete runway. Every five seconds or so it dropped me so that my backside hit the concrete and searing flames shot through my body...Ahead of me I heard two violent explosions, and then I hit the ground and skidded for about half a dozen feet, then lay there gasping on my back as the small parachute sank down on me like a deflated balloon. I didn't know it then but the pilot had jammed the brakes on to shorten my torture and, possibly, save my life.

I had no idea of how far the plane had skidded down the runway, although later I was told that it had been 400 yards. All I knew was that I felt sick and shaken to the marrow, but I struggled into a sitting position. My backside felt like a roasted chunk of T-bone steak.

* * * *

Daniel Minne had been lucky, and he lived to tell the tale. But another paratrooper, Lieutenant Kurt Angele, was even more fortunate. In July 1957, Angele was taking part in a mass drop by Federal German paratroops at Oberhausen, West Germany, in front of some assembled press photographers, who in the event got more than they anticipated.

The first aircraft (also a Noratlas) flew over the dropping zone at 1500 feet. A series of black specks tumbled from it and their parachutes blossomed out – all except one. The leading jumper plummeted earthwards with only a thin ribbon of parachute trailing after him. Before anyone had time to register horror, his body hit the ground. The Pressmen were kept well away. They made for the nearest telephones, anxious to get the story to their papers before their deadlines. The early headlines said: 'Paratrooper killed in air exercise.' They were somewhat premature.

Twenty-one-year old Angele had only recently been awarded his paratrooper's brevet, and was leading his men into action on manoeuvres for the first time. They had sacks filled with 100 pounds of sand strapped to the lower part of their bodies to simulate the weight of equipment they would have to carry in real combat. As he moved to his jump position, Angele found that the strap which held his sandbag in position just above his knees was cutting painfully into him. Contrary to orders, he loosened it.

Almost as soon as he jumped, Angele knew that something had gone dreadfully wrong. Loosening his load had been a mistake; it was now off balance and causing him to roll over and over. There was a crack as the static line pulled his parachute pack open. The parachute started to stream, but the shroud lines wound themselves round his spinning body like a spider's web. He had no idea how close he was to the ground; his only sensations were of earth and sky whirling around him and the blast of the wind against him.

He was on his back when he thudded almost two feet deep into the soft ground at a speed estimated later as ninety mph. Angele was still conscious. He felt no pain, just a burning sensation, as if all the blood in his body had concentrated in his back. His tongue began to swell until it seemed to reach a monstrous size, choking him. He fought for breath, unable to move.

Angele was lifted from the hole and carried to an ambulance. In hospital, doctors found that seven ribs were broken, one lung torn, two vertebrae were broken with splinters threatening to penetrate the spinal marrow and his right kidney was crushed. The doctors saw no prospect of his survival, but they did what they could, and Angela lived. Nine weeks after his accident, he was well enough to get out of bed, and in November 1958 he reported back to his unit, although his days as a paratrooper were over. Later, he was promoted to the rank of major and given a staff job at the German Army Sports Training Centre, Warendorf.

He made one more parachute jump, for two reasons. The first was to show that he could conquer his fear; the second was to prove that he could make as perfect a parachute descent as possible. He was successful on both counts.

* * * *

Kurt Angele had had no opportunity to deploy his reserve parachute, unlike a skydiver who was involved in an extraordinary incident in 1975. It happened in Derbyshire, four people surviving when they and a Cessna 182 light aircraft descended from 2000 feet under a single Irvin I.24 reserve parachute, similar to that used by glider pilots, sport parachutists and service aircrew.

The aircraft was flying over the Ashbourne dropping zone on a training sortie from the Peak Sports Parachute Club. The first trainee had dropped successfully, but the second, who was using a static line and making his first jump, slipped forward as he stepped on to the starboard wheel and became wedged between the wheel and the strut. Before he could be freed, he pulled his reserve parachute, which deployed and caused the aircraft to stall. The canopy inflated successfully, leaving the aircraft inverted and the trainee suspended between canopy and Cessna.

At this point the 182 contained the pilot, a third trainee (a girl) and an instructor. The aircraft eventually struck the ground inverted, with the parachutist above it landing safely, his only injury a strained back. The most serious injuries to the occupants were a broken jaw and two fractured thighbones; the Cessna was rather more permanently damaged.

* * * *

It would be hard to imagine a more dangerous parachute descent than that made by a US Marine Corps pilot, Lieutenant-Colonel William Rankin, on 26 July 1959. Rankin was flying a Vought F8U *Crusader*, accompanied by a second aircraft flown by Lieutenant Herbert Nolan, on a transit flight from Massachusetts to Beaufort, South Carolina when trouble struck without warning. The two aircraft had climbed to 47,000 feet to clear an unusually high thunderstorm in the vicinity of Norfolk, Virginia, when Rankin felt and heard a thump and a rumbling sound behind and beneath his cockpit. Quickly, he scanned his instruments. He was flying at Mach 0.82 and nothing seemed to be wrong, but then he heard the thump and rumble again and his fire warning light flashed on.

His first instinct was to reduce power. Then he called Nolan, advising him that he was having engine trouble and might be forced to eject. The fire warning light went out, but the engine rpm indicator was unwinding rapidly as power dropped away, the engine speed falling from about ninety per cent to zero in five or six seconds. Rankin knew without any doubt that something had caused the engine to seize, and without the engine he had no electrical power or hydraulics. Without hydraulic assistance it became impossible to move the control column.

Rankin reached to his left and pulled the handle that actuated the emergency power turbine. Nothing happened. He pulled again, and the handle came right out of the cockpit wall.

There was nothing more I could do, Rankin recalled later. Without power, I could not dive to a lower, safer level for ejection. Nor could I stay with the plane much longer, for it might stall and fall into a wild spin. But no one, so far as I knew, had ever ejected at this altitude, at any speed, with or without a pressure suit or some protective clothing. The temperature outside was seventy degrees below zero, and I was wearing only a summer-weight flying suit, gloves, helmet and ordinary shoes. Perhaps I could survive frostbite without permanent injury, but what about decompression? I was almost ten miles up, where the air is so thin that the blood in a man's body, lacking the shield of a pressure suit, could literally come to the boil, if the skin was punctured.

A Vought F8U Crusader of the type flown by Lieutenant Commander Rankin. (LTV)

The massive, rolling thunderstorms below him were frightening. Some years earlier, Rankin had flown into a thunderstorm in a piston-engined F4U Corsair fighter-bomber. The turbulence that hit the aircraft was so violent that it had turned the F4U over on its back, and Rankin had barely managed to regain control. There was no time to dwell on that now. He reached up, grasped the handle of the ejection seat's face blind and pulled hard.

Rankin's first sensation was one of severe cold and extreme expansion, as if he were about to explode. The cold rapidly changed to a burning, tingling sensation. He felt as if millions of pins were sticking in. Then, seconds later, the painful tingling gave way to a blessed numbness. He opened his eyes and saw that he was entering wispy clouds, the tops of the fleecy overcast through which he had flown just a few minutes earlier. He remembered that the altitude had been 44,000 feet.

> At the same time I felt the almost unbearable pain of decompression. I could feel my abdomen distending, stretching, until I thought it would give way. My eyes felt as though they were ripped from their sockets, my ears seemed to to be bursting, my entire body was racked by cramps. Once I caught a horrified glimpse of my abdomen swollen as though I were in well-advanced pregnancy. I had never known such savage pain in my life.

Strangely, Rankin had no immediate sensation of falling, only of spinning like a pinwheel, with his arms and legs trying to go in all directions at once. Brilliant colours rotated against a purplish void, with the sun sweeping past in streaks of blurred reddish-orange. Despite his predicament, the pilot felt a surge of elation with the realisation that he was still alive.

> I had the feeling that I fell and fell and fell and fell for an eternity. My oxygen mask was beating against my face. I held my mask with my right hand. I put my left hand on my helmet which was pulling on the chin strap as if it was going to go off. My left hand was very cold and numb – it felt like somebody else's hand, not mine.
>
> Some time during the free fall, my right glove got in my way. It inflated like a balloon so I let it go – just jettisoned it. During the free fall I had the feeling of not being able to exhale; in fact, I seemed to have to work very hard to be able to exhale, but all I had to do was open my mouth and in-rushing air just seemed to fill my lungs. At this time it was getting a bit darker in the cloud. I had an urge to open the parachute but I told myself I was still far too high and if I did I would either freeze to death or die from lack of oxygen. I still had this tingling sensation but I sort of had the feeling that I was slowing down and falling into denser atmosphere and I seemed to be getting a little warmer.
>
> I was still in the free fall and thinking about opening the chute. It was quite dark but I don't recall any great moisture or any great violence. It seems like while I was thinking about opening the chute, all of a sudden there was a terrific jolt and I knew the chute had opened. I looked up but by this time I was in such a dense, dark cloud that I couldn't even see my

canopy. I reached up and got hold of the risers and gave them tugs on both sides; it felt like I had a good chute. From here on, my memory of what happened seems much better. I now clearly recall running out of oxygen, having the mask collapse against my face, and I believe I disconnected it from the right side as I always do. At about this time I thought I definitely had it made and was going to survive. However, I noticed I was still bleeding from the nose, my right hand was cut, and my left hand was frozen numb, but the pressure was going and I was much more comfortable. Then the turbulence started and I realised I was entering the thunderstorm.

As the turbulence started, I was pelted all over by hail. Then I fell a little bit more and I seemed to be caught in a violent updraft. I had the feeling that I was being tossed around – that I was actually going around in a loop and I was looping over my canopy like being on the end of a centrifuge. I got sick in the turbulence and heaved. Sometimes I could see the canopy and sometimes I couldn't. The tossing and the turbulence was so violent it is difficult to describe. I went up and down – I was buffeted about in all directions – at times it felt like I was going sideways. One time I hit a very rough blast of air – I went soaring back up and got in a very severe hailstorm. I remember the hail beating down on my helmet. I had the feeling it would tear my canopy up. The next thing I knew I was in rain so heavy I felt like I was standing under a waterfall. I had my mask loose and the water was so great that when I tried to inhale I got water with the air like I was swimming. It seems to me that some time in the storm I noticed my watch and was surprised that it had stayed with me. I'm not sure but I think I was able to tell the time by the luminous dial – I believe it was around 1815.

At one time during an up or down draft, the parachute canopy collapsed and came down over me like a big sheet. I could see my legs in the shroud lines. This gave me some concern – I thought maybe the chute wouldn't blossom again properly and since the hail seemed to be larger now I was afraid it might damage the canopy and put holes in it. I fell and the canopy blossomed again. I felt the risers and everything seemed all right. At this time I looked down and saw what appeared to be a big black elevator shaft. Then I felt like I had been hit by a blast of compressed air and I went soaring back up again – up and down – sideways. How much of this soaring went on I don't know. I had the feeling that if it went on much longer I was not going to maintain consciousness. I was being tossed around and beaten around and I wasn't quite sure how much more I could take. The violence was so great that I thought that if it doesn't stop soon, my gear will come apart – and my straps will break – I will come apart. Stretching – twisting – slamming – the turbulence of this thunderstorm was so violent I have nothing to compare it with. I became quite airsick and I had considerable vertigo. Again I had the feeling that I couldn't take much more of this *but if I could only hold out a little while longer, I would be falling out of the roughest part of the storm.*

The lightning was so severe that I kept my eyes closed most of the time. Even with my eyelids closed, there was a blinding reddish-white light when the lightning flashed. I felt rather than heard the thunder; it just about burst my eardrums. As I recall, I had the feeling that I was in the upper part of the storm because the lightning seemed to be just flashes. As I descended, I seemed to see big red streaks heading towards the earth. All of a sudden I realised it was getting a little calmer and I was probably descending below the storm. The turbulence grew less, then ceased and I realised I was below the storm. The rain continued, the air was smooth, and I started thinking about my landing.

By now my shoulders and legs hurt pretty badly. I checked myself over again and thought I was O.K. I kept looking down and said to myself 'Under the storm you probably won't have more than three hundred feet.' It was just like breaking out when you're making a GCA [ground controlled approach]. The first thing I saw was green and then I was able to see trees and then I knew I was very close to the deck. I remember seeing a field off in the distance and I thought there must be people nearby. As I got close to the trees I suddenly realised there was a surface wind and I was being carried horizontally over the ground quite rapidly – maybe 25 knots. I oscillated about three times, then went into the trees. It seemed that my chute fouled in two pine trees and I continued in a horizontal position with the wind, then swung back to the left. I came crashing back through the trees like a pendulum and hit a large tree with my left side. My head, face, and shoulder took most of the blow. My helmet was knocked crooked but I think it did a great deal to save me here. The blow was so violent that it twisted my helmet back on the right side and pulled the chin strap so tight over my Adam's apple under my chin that I had to loosen it when I got on the ground. Anyway, I came down with a crash. I slid down and landed on my side. I was cold and stunned but still conscious. At first I thought I had broken something and was paralysed. Pretty soon, however, I was able to move my head and then my arms. I checked the time; it was between 1840 and 1845.

Pulling himself together as best he could, shaking and shivering, Rankin released himself from his parachute and, jungle knife in hand, stumbled through a tangle of underbrush until he reached a cornfield. Over the tops of the cornstalks he could see the headlights of moving cars. Struggling through the corn, he reached the edge of the road.

Several cars passed me, ignoring my shouts and frantic gestures. I must have been a terrifying sight standing there in the purplish twilight in my tattered flight suit and helmet, with a large knife in my hand, blood caked on my face and oozing out of my mouth, nose and ears. Finally, as a car went by, I sank to my knees. About fifty yards down the road, I saw its red brake lights go on. It turned and came back. The driver

Another Crusader pilot who had a lucky escape was Lieutenant (jg) John T. Kryway of VF-11 'Red Rippers', who was operating from the carrier Franklin Delano Roosevelt off Dominica in October 1961. A rough landing, caused by a sudden dip as the aircraft was touching down, caused the starboard wheel to break off. It punctured the main fuel line and the aircraft, catching fire, hurtled down the flight deck and plunged over the side. Kryway ejected successfully and his parachute deployed just before he hit the water. He survived with only minor injuries. (US Navy)

motioned me into the front seat. He was Judson Dunning, a farmer, with his wife, three young sons and a teenage cousin. I asked where we were. Near Rich Square, North Carolina, he said. That was some seventy miles from Norfolk.

Rankin spent two weeks under constant observation in the Beaufort Base Hospital, where a small army of specialists found to their amazement that the pilot had suffered no serious damage, apart from severe bruising, lacerations, a badly cut finger, generalised swelling (especially of the eyelids), slight haemorrhage in one eye, some early difficulty in focusing on small print, widespread discolouration of the skin due to frostbite, and sprains and strains of ligaments, joints and muscles. He went on to make a complete recovery, and returned to flying duties.

CHAPTER THIRTEEN

VIETNAM

For the United States, the Vietnam War was a costly business, in terms of both men and material. In the case of the US Navy, seventeen attack carriers made seventy-three combat cruises off Vietnam between August 1964 and August 1973, losing 530 fixed-wing aircraft, thirteen helicopters and 317 aircrew. The US Air Force, whose operations in Vietnam extended from October 1961 to March 1973, lost 2257 aircraft, with 2118 aircrew killed and 599 missing. The aircraft losses included thirty Boeing B-52 Stratofortresses, half of which were destroyed on just a week of operations at the end of 1972.

In the latter stages of the Vietnam War the B-52s had a taste of how effective Soviet air defence weaponry could be. It happened during Operation Linebacker II, a strategic bombing offensive against North Vietnam which was authorised by President Richard M. Nixon in May 1972 against the background of a major North Vietnamese Army offensive against the south and a stalemate at the Paris peace talks. As part of the offensive, B-52s ventured into heavily defended North Vietnamese air space for the first time in May and June to make limited night attacks on airfields and oil storage facilities, and also to lay mines in the waters of Haiphong and other strategic ports. These minelaying operations, carried out by modified B-52Ds, were also flown under cover of darkness, and no losses were sustained.

On 20 October 1972, when it seemed as though the Paris talks were at last leading to an agreement that would end the war, air operations over North Vietnam were once more halted. They were resumed when the peace talks again broke down amid indications that the North Vietnamese were preparing to renew their offensive in the south. There followed an eleven-day bombing campaign against the north which developed into the heaviest bombing offensive of the war, with round-the-clock attacks on targets which had mostly been on the restricted list until then. They included rail yards, power plants, communications facilities, petrol, oil and lubrication (POL) stores and ammunition supply dumps, as well as the principal North Vietnamese Air Force (NVAF) fighter bases and SAM sites. The target list numbered thirty-four strategic objectives, over sixty per cent of which were situated within a twenty-five-mile radius of Hanoi.

The original plan called for the B-52s to attack at night, in three waves, with F-111s and A-6s continuing the offensive in daylight. The B-52 bomber streams were to be preceded by F-111 interdictors, attacking fighter bases at low level, and F-4 Phantoms dropping *Window* (metallic strips designed to confuse enemy radar). The B-52s were to approach their target areas from the north-west, using strong high-altitude winds to give them a much increased

The mighty B-52, designed for a nuclear strike, paid a heavy price in its conventional bombing operations over North Vietnam. (USAF)

ground speed, and after bomb release they were to swing away from the target in tight turns in order to clear SAM defences as quickly as possible. Attacks would be made by cells of three aircraft, generally bombing from 33,000 feet. The three aircraft were to fly in close formation to pool their electronic countermeasures (ECM) resources, which included the GE ALQ-87 and ITT ALQ-117 jammers and the Lundy ALE-24 chaff dispensing system.

The operation began on the night of 18/19 December 1972, when 129 B-52s took off from their respective bases in Thailand and on Guam. Thirty minutes before the first cells arrived over their targets, F-111s carried out strikes on enemy airfields and F-4s sowed two chaff corridors to screen the attacks on the target areas of Kinh No and Yen Vien, north of Hanoi. Unfortunately, the strong north-west wind had dispersed the chaff before the B-52s arrived. The first B-52 wave to attack the Yen Vien rail yards flew over a cluster of SAM sites as it began its final run-in to the target, and Charcoal 1 – the leading aircraft in the 'Charcoal' cell – sustained a near miss from an SA-2 just as its bomb doors were opening. Crippled and out of control, with its pilot, co-pilot and gunner either dead or incapacitated, the bomber began its long plunge to earth. The navigator, radar navigator and electronic warfare officer ejected and were taken prisoners. A second B-52, attacking with 'Peach' cell in the second wave four hours later, was luckier; it was also crippled by an SA-2, this time just after completing its bombing run, but managed to reach friendly territory with wing and engine fires before its crew were forced to abandon it. The third wave of eighteen B-52s, attacking five hours later, encountered fierce opposition over the target (the Hanoi railway repair shops). More than sixty SAM launches were observed, but the bombers' ECM worked well and there were no losses, although one aircraft was damaged by a near miss. Another wave of twenty-one aircraft, attacking from the west, also encountered heavy opposition from eleven SAM sites in the Hanoi area and lost the leading aircraft in the last cell to bomb, Rose 1. On this first night of Linebacker II, therefore, in which the enemy had launched more than 200 SAMs and expended massive quantities of AAA ammunition, the SA-2s had destroyed three B-52s and damaged three more.

The B-52s suffered no casualties on the night of 19/20 December, when 120 bombers attacked several targets in the Hanoi area. However, the North Vietnamese had by now realised that the bombers were approaching their target areas along the same tracks each night, and they evolved new tactics that included sending up MiGs to shadow the incoming bomber stream and verify its altitude, so that the defences could fuze their missile warheads and AAA shells accordingly. During the third night of operations, on 20/21 December, SA-2s knocked down two B-52s as they completed their bombing runs, and both of them crashed in Hanoi. A third B-52, badly damaged, struggled back to Thailand, only to crash on landing, killing four of its crew. Two more B-52s in the last wave that night were destroyed by SAMs; a third was crippled and crashed in Laos. In the nine hour operation the enemy had fired 220 SAMs and claimed six B-52s, four of which were B-52Gs.

On the fourth night, 21/22 December, the tactics employed by the bomber stream were modified. The time between attacking waves was greatly reduced, attacking altitudes were varied and the cells were randomly spaced. In addition, individual crews were given freedom of action in evasive manoeuvring; most favoured a shallow post-attack turn followed by a dive to low altitude and a high-speed run clear of the Vietnamese defences over the Gulf of Tonkin. All sorties on this night were flown from U-Tapao, the Guam-based B-52s being released for *Arc Light* missions (carpet-bombing

A B-52 being bombed-up at Andersen Air Base, Guam, for a mission over Vietnam.
(USAF)

attacks on suspected North Vietnamese Army troop movements in the south) and there were no losses. The B-52 force was stood down for thirty-six hours over the Christmas period, but on the night of 26/27 December 120 B-52s, flying in tightly compressed waves and accompanied by 113 defence suppression and ECM aircraft, attacked ten targets in Hanoi, Haiphong and Thai Nguyen, the more vulnerable B-52Gs being assigned to the latter objectives. Two streams attacked Hanoi from the north-west, flying in from Laos and out over the Gulf of Tonkin, while two more attacked on a reciprocal track. All the bombers passed through the target areas within fifteen minutes and only one B-52 fell to the SAM defences, although a second, severely damaged, crashed short of the runway while attempting an emergency landing in Thailand.

This aircraft, a B-52D from the 307th Strategic Wing based at U-Tapao, Thailand, piloted by Captain John D. Mize, had an epic struggle for survival from the moment it flew into shoals of SA-2 missiles on the approach to Hanoi. By this time the North Vietnamese air defences were severely degraded and the remaining stocks of SA-2s were being salvo-launched blindly, but a missile was still deadly if it passed close enough to a target to detonate its warhead's proximity fuze, and this is exactly what happened to Mize's B-52.

As he approached the target area, Mize saw at least fifteen SA-2s in the air, and ten seconds after the B-52 had released its load of eighty-four 500 pound bombs it was shaken by a tremendous explosion on the port side. Mize felt red-hot shrapnel slice into his left thigh and lower left leg, and his right had, resting on the control column, was lacerated by flying splinters. The tail gunner, T/Sgt Peter E. Whalen, and the navigator, Lt Bill Robinson, were also wounded, but not incapacitated.

Abruptly, the B-52's lights and electrical systems went out. The huge bomber lurched to the left, then to the right. Mize was thrown forward against his harness. Engine and fire warning lights, flashing on the instrument panel, told him that three of the bomber's turbojets were out of action and that a fourth was on the verge of quitting, all of them on the same side of the aircraft.

Mize managed to regain control with the help of is co-pilot, Captain Terrance Gauthers, and called each crew member in turn to check on their status. Navigator Bill Robinson gave him a course to steer for Nakhon Phanom, the nearest air base in Thailand, but there was only a very remote chance that the crippled bomber might reach it. It was buffeting and shaking, flying on four of its eight engines, and it was on fire, acting like a beacon to any North Vietnamese night fighters in the vicinity.

The B-52 staggered on to the border with Laos, where it was met by a Lockheed HC-130 Hercules rescue co-ordination aircraft, alerted by Mize's distress call. The bomber was at 12,000 feet over mountainous terrain; Robinson told the pilot that if they could keep going for another thirty miles, they would be over much flatter terrain where it would be safer to eject.

Things were starting to go badly wrong now as the B-52's systems began to fail. The bomb bay doors fell open, one landing gear unit started to cycle up and down, and the electric systems were running amok. Mize knew that he was losing control rapidly, and ordered the crew to eject. Four of them did so, including the co-pilot and the radar navigator, Captain Bill North. The other navigator, Bill Robinson, pulled the handle of his downward-ejecting seat and nothing happened. Unstrapping himself from the seat, he dropped into the night through the hatchway that had been opened up when Bill North ejected.

Mize waited for a few seconds, giving Robinson time to get out, then ejected himself. All six crew members landed safely, operated their radio beacons and were picked up by the rescue helicopters which had been following the bomber in its final minutes, guided by the HC-130. Captain Mize was later awarded a well-earned Air Force Cross.

The last three nights of Linebacker II, in which sixty B-52s were committed on each night, cost Strategic Air Command (SAC) five more bombers, all victims of SAMs. By this time the North Vietnamese defences had been virtually neutralised, and the enemy had expended most of their stock of about 1,000 SA-2s. On 30 December, North Vietnam announced that it was ready to resume peace negotiations. In all, 729 B-52 sorties had been flown during Linebacker II, and more than 15,000 tons of bombs dropped. Fifteen B-52s had been lost to the SAM defences, and nine damaged. Thirty-four targets had been hit, and some 1,500 civilians killed. Of the ninety-two crew members aboard the shot-down bombers, twenty-six were recovered by rescue teams, twenty-nine were listed as missing, and thirty-three baled out over North Vietnam to be taken prisoner and later repatriated.

CHAPTER FOURTEEN

LOW, FAST AND FURIOUS

The change of operational tactics from high- to low-level attack in the early 1960s, following the increasing sophistication of hostile air defence systems, threw up a whole new set of crew escape problems. Particularly affected were aircraft like the Lockheed F-104 Starfighter, which had a downwards-ejecting seat, and arrangement that was to cost a great many lives during that type's long and troubled career. In the early days of the XF-104 programme, it was decided that, due to the limitations of the available ejection seat catapults, the ejection seat should fire downwards. This was seen as the best means of enabling the pilot to clear the aircraft structure, especially the vertical fin at higher speeds, and also reducing the effect of wind blast on the pilot. Later, these Lockheed C-1 seats were replaced by the upward-firing C-2. These seats served well in USAF service, but were still not considered suitable for extreme low-level ejections with high sink rates. This was a particular problem for the German Luftwaffe and other NATO air forces, which used the F-104G model in the low-level strike role. Eventually, after many pilots hd been lost, the F-104G was re-equipped with a seat of Martin-Baker design.

In some aircraft types, a solution to the problem of low-level egress at supersonic speed was sought by the provision of crew escape capsules, rather than individual ejection seats. When the supersonic Convair B-58 Hustler entered service with the US Strategic Air Command in 1961, it originally had individual ejection seats for its three crew members. However, ejection at speeds above 665 mph was extremely hazardous, and to improve ejection survivability, the Stanley Aircraft Corporation developed a high-speed capsule ejection system that would allow safe ejection at supersonic speed. The capsule was adopted for retrofit beginning in late 1962, making the B-58 the first USAF aircraft with a capsule ejection system. It was effective throughout the flight envelope up to 70,000 feet and twice the speed of sound.

The capsule had airtight clamshell doors and independent pressurisation and oxygen supply systems, with survival gear packed inside. Raising a handgrip activated the restraint harness system, securing the occupant inside and closing the capsule doors. The crew member could then initiate the ejection procedure by squeezing an ejection trigger, to be catapulted out of the aircraft in his rocket-assisted capsule. The pilot's capsule contained a control column and other essential controls so that he could continue to fly the aircraft while encapsulated. After ejection, a parachute lowered the capsule and shock absorbers eased its impact on touchdown. In the event of a water landing the capsule was able to float, and was fitted with additional flotation cells that could be manually inflated, providing stability and turning the capsule into a life raft.

An escape capsule, in this case enclosing both crew members, was also fitted to the General Dynamics F-111; or, to be rather more accurate, the whole cockpit doubled as an escape capsule which separated completely from the aircraft, being blown clear by a rocket motor. The pilot and weapon systems officer (WSO) sat side-by-side in a shirt-sleeve environment, wearing no pressure suits or oxygen masks. If they decided to eject, the first step in the sequence was to fire a bunch of explosive guillotines that severed all the hydraulic lines and cables. Then, a large rocket propellant charge separated the entire cockpit from the aircraft. When it separated, the ejection capsule took with it a small portion of the fuselage above and to the rear of the cockpit which acted as a stabilising aerofoil. After the parachutes opened, anti-radar chaff was dispersed, and a cushion/flotation bag was inflated to soften the impact when the capsule landed. All of this could be accomplished from zero/zero airspeed/altitude – in other words, from an aircraft parked motionless on a runway. In the case of an over-water ejection, the capsule was supposed to be completely submersible and was capable of floating for a considerable amount of time. While the capsule was floating in the water, the control column could double as a bilge pump by moving a pin in its base.

The escape capsule was used with success, although on several occasions crew members were injured following a hard landing.

The Rockwell B-1A supersonic variable-geometry jet bomber featured an escape capsule resembling the F-111's, but designed to hold four crew members. Once clear of the aircraft, the capsule would be lowered under three parachutes, and once on the ground it would serve as a survival shelter for the crew. The B-1A programme was abandoned by President Jimmy Carter's administration, but the aircraft was resurrected as the B-1B under President Ronal Reagan. The two B-1A prototypes were both used in the B-1B test programme and one of these crashed on 29 August 1984 when the aircraft's centre of gravity shifted during fuel transfer as it manoeuvred on two engines, causing it to lose control. The escape capsule ejected successfully, but the parachute risers did not deploy properly. The capsule hit the ground at a steep angle, so steep that the inflatable cushions could not shield the impact. Chief test pilot Doug Benefield was killed, and two other crew members were seriously injured.

Operational B-1Bs were fitted with the conventional rocket-propelled zero-zero ACES II ejection seat. ACES (Advanced Concept Ejection Seat) is derived from the Douglas Escapac seat and is the standard USAF Government Furnished Aerospace Equipment (GFAE) ejection seat, being used in the F-15, F-16, B-1, B-2, F-117, A-10 and F-22 aircraft.

Although the Douglas Escapac seat was developed for use in some US naval aircraft like the Douglas A-4 Skyhawk, Vought A-7 Corsair II and Lockheed S-3 Viking, the US Navy has traditionally opted for the British Martin-Baker

The pilot of a 'Thunderbirds' US Air Force aerobatic team F-16 uses his ACES II seat to eject at low level after his aircraft suffered a technical failure at an air show in the USA. (USAF/Staff Sgt Davis)

range of seats. By 2005 Martin-Baker had produced some 68,000 seats for air forces around the world, starting with the Mk 1. At the time of writing, some 7000 lives have been saved by the use of Martin-Baker seats. The Company's more recent ejection seat designs, such as the Mk 10 series, use an on-board electronic sequencer to sense various factors such as speed and altitude to optimise control of the seat's operation. Emergency ejections have been made under conditions ranging from ground level to the highest at 57,000 feet, and from a standstill to an indicated airspeed of over 800 mph.

The latest Mk 16 range of seats has been selected against strong competition for the Raytheon T-6A, Korean Aerospace's KT-1 and T-50, Pilatus PC-21, Northrop T-38 and F-5, Aermacchi M-346, Dassault Rafale and the Eurofighter Typhoon. Martin-Baker is currently developing the next generation ejection seat for the F-35 Joint Strike Fighter.

The Russian company Zvezda is probably Martin-Baker's biggest rival. Zvezda produces both the K-36D ejection seat fitted to the MiG-29 and SU-27 aircraft and the K-37 helicopter ejection seat fitted to the Ka-50 Havoc.

Seats like the K-36D and the M-B Mk 16 have brought ejection seat development to its apex, but there is a new frontier waiting to be explored. It lies in earth's orbit, where there exists, as yet, no effective means of escape for the crew of a crippled spacecraft.

INDEX